# Legal Rights for Seniors

## A Guide to Health Care, Income Benefits and Senior Legal Services

**Author:** Wesley J. Smith
**Editor:** Kay Ostberg
**Project Director:** Theresa Meehan Rudy
**Graphics & Production:** David Bell
**Substantial Assistance Provided By:** Joseph Brown,
Danielle Hager, Caleen Norrod and Barbara Stillman

Our thanks to the following consumer specialists, organizations and
attorneys for their invaluable comments and advice: Alvin D. Hersh, Legal
Counsel for the Elderly, Arlene Lilly, Patricia McGinnis, Choice In Dying,
Pension Rights Center and Gregory Wilcox.

First Edition: April, 1993

ISBN 0-910073-17-1

# TABLE OF
# CONTENTS

## PART 3   MISCELLANEOUS SENIOR SERVICES & LEGAL RIGHTS

## APPENDICES

# INTRODUCTION

Senior citizens, like the rest of society, are increasingly finding themselves caught-up in the complexities of modern life. Everything has become so fast-paced, so complicated, and yes, so legalistic. The rules of government programs can be daunting and the law surrounding a wide variety of issues of concern to seniors, ranging from estate planning to receiving quality medical care, can be intimidating and confusing. The purpose of this book is to shine a bright light through the red tape known as "elder law."

Elder law is a growing field of law that is of increasing importance to senior citizens. It is important that you understand and use the legal knowledge you will gain from this book, for by doing so, you will develop a better understanding of your rights.

## A WORD ABOUT TERMS

You don't need a law degree to use this book and understand its contents. Yet, a discussion of the law invariably must use legal words and phrases that lawyers call "terms of art." Every time a new legal term or phrase is used in this book, it is printed in italics. A glossary (Appendix 3) has been included at the end of the book to assist you.

## HOW TO USE THIS BOOK

Designed as a reference text, this book can be read from cover-to-cover, but its most important use will be as a resource during a time of need. For example, if you have a question about Medicare coverage and hospitalization, the book can answer your questions and tell you where to go if you need more details. In fact, within these pages you should be able to find a discussion of most legal problems that relate specifically to your needs as a senior citizen.

The book is divided into three separate parts. The first deals with medical care. There, you will find chapters on *Medicare, Medicaid,* and health insurance for seniors to supplement Medicare (known as *Medigap*) among other topics. The second part deals with your income. *Social Security* benefits are described, *pensions* are discussed and ways you can use the *equity* value of your property, to increase the money in your pocket. The final section covers a wide variety of topics, from your rights as a nursing home resident to age discrimination to funeral arrangements.

## DEALING WITH PROFESSIONALS

Although this book gives a general description of the law; it cannot give you legal advice based on your individual circumstances. However, most of the time, the information you receive in these pages should be sufficient for you to understand your rights and conduct your affairs from a position of knowledge and insight. Problem areas are flagged where you might need professional advice or assistance. You may also wish to explore other books that give more details about a particular subject. Additional resources are listed in the bibliography (Appendix 4).

# PART 1

# YOUR
# HEALTH CARE

# *1*

# A PROFILE
# OF MEDICARE

Senior citizens have long been interested in obtaining government financial assistance to help pay for quality health care at a reasonable price. President Truman first seriously proposed a national health insurance system for senior citizens. But the program was not easily born. It took years of political action and grass-roots efforts, similar to the current effort to create a form of universal national health insurance, before the country finally decided that after a lifetime of productivity and contribution to society, seniors were entitled to Medicare. Thus, it wasn't until July 1, 1966, that the program was born.

Since then, Medicare has become a fact of senior life. It is so important to your financial well-being that we have devoted the first three chapters of this book to the topic and a fourth to the important issue of private insurance to supplement Medicare coverage. In the coming pages, we will describe the program, revealing which health costs are covered and those which are not. We will also detail your out-of-pocket costs under Medicare and will reveal the fine print that can cost you money or reduce your coverage. And, we'll describe available alternatives to Medicare.

We start with a general overview of Medicare. It is a form of national health insurance that is designed primarily, but not exclusively, to benefit those of you who are age 65 and over. Its purpose is to assist you to pay for your medical bills, not pay for all of your medical needs. The hospitals, doctors and other health-care providers who treat Medicare recipients are not employed by the government. Rather, they are members of the private sector health care community who have agreed to accept Medicare benefits as partial payment for their services.

Medicare is administered and financed exclusively by the Federal Government, through the offices of the Health Care Financing Administration, which is part of the U. S. Department of Health and Human Services. However, applications and information about the program are easily obtained at your local *Social Security Administration* office. (To find the office nearest you, look in the governmental listings of your local telephone book.)

Medicare is a national program. This is important because it allows the rules of coverage and eligibility to apply equally throughout the country. Thus, people eligible for coverage in Alabama are also eligible in California, and beneficiaries of the program may move anywhere in the United States without worrying that they will lose Medicare benefits or have to wait for renewed eligibility.

Medicare benefits apply across a broad range of health care needs, such as hospitalization and medical treatment. The next two chapters will discuss each of these areas in detail. You also need to know about those areas of health care that are not covered by Medicare. For example, Medicare does not pay for services known as *custodial care*. Thus, seniors who must be admitted to nursing homes for long-term care will not receive Medicare benefits to help pay their costs (see Chapter 2).

Medicare is divided into two general parts, *Part A* and *Part B*. Part A is designed to help you pay for the costs of hospitalization. Also, Part A may cover treatment in a skilled nursing facility, home health care, hospice services and blood transfusions. Part B pays for most "outpatient" medical services, such as your doctor's fees, ambulance services, administered drugs (as opposed to prescription drugs), medical equipment and supplies, and outpatient physical or speech therapy. Part A will be discussed in detail in Chapter 2, and Part B will be dealt with in Chapter 3.

Now let's turn to some specifics. For the balance of this chapter, we will detail significant issues such as eligibility, how to enroll, trading Medicare benefits for membership in a *health maintenance organization* (HMO), and other important topics of general concern.

## WHO IS ELIGIBLE FOR MEDICARE?

The first topic we will tackle is the most basic question of who is eligible to join the program. Please note that the two different parts of Medicare, Part A and Part B, have different eligibility criteria.

### Part A

If you are age 65 or over, you are probably eligible for Medicare. If any of the following statements is true about you, you are automatically entitled to *free* Part A coverage:

**You receive retirement under the Social Security or Railroad Retirement systems.** If you elected to receive retirement benefits before your 65th birthday, your Medicare card will come automatically in the mail, when you turn 65. You are not eligible for Medicare if you are under age 65, even if you are receiving Social Security Retirement Benefits.

**You are eligible for Social Security retirement benefits but have not applied for them.** If you are eligible to receive retirement benefits (see Chapter 9), but have chosen not to take them, you must *apply* for Medicare Part A in order to be covered. *Note:* It is a good idea to apply about three months before you turn 65 so that you will be covered as soon as you celebrate your birthday. If you apply within six months of your 65th birthday, coverage will date-back to your 65th birthday. If you wait longer, your benefits will only date-back for six months after you apply.

**You are under 65 years old and are disabled or need kidney dialysis.** Free Part A coverage is also available to a limited number of people who are under age 65. If you receive continuing dialysis for permanent kidney failure or have had a kidney transplant you are as eligible, as are people who have received Social Security disability benefits for twenty-four months. For more information, contact your local Social Security office.

### Part A Can Be Purchased If You're Not Eligible

Most of you who are reading these words will qualify for Medicare through quarters of coverage (sometimes referred to as work credits) earned in the Social Security program (see Chapter 8). However, even if you do not qualify for Social Security and you are age 65 or older, you can "buy into" the system by purchasing your coverage as if it were an insurance policy. To do this, you must apply between January 1 and March 31 of the year. The amount of premium you will pay will be set by Congress each year. In 1993, it was $221 per month.

Once you have successfully applied for Part A coverage, your benefits will begin on July 1 of the year you enroll. *Note:* If you fail to enroll within one year of eligibility, you may have to pay a ten percent premium surcharge for each year after age 65 you wait to apply.

### Part B

Part B coverage is available to anyone who is age 65 or over, is a United States citizen or who has lived legally in the United States for five consecutive years. This is true whether or not you qualify for Part A coverage through Social Security quarters or work credits.

You must pay for Part B coverage and you can expect the price of coverage to go up every year. (In 1993, it cost $36.60 per month for most beneficiaries.) You are well advised to sign up for the program because, as you will see in Chapter 3, it covers a wide range of medical care. If you have been signed up under Part A, you will be automatically enrolled in Part B, and your premium will be deducted from your Social Security or Railroad Retirement monthly payment. (If you don't want Part B, you must notify your Social Security office.)

There are two different Part B enrollment periods that you need to know about:

The *"initial enrollment period"* is available to you for a seven-month period, beginning three months before the month of your 65th birthday and ending three months after the end of the month of your 65th birthday. This sounds like a mouth full of bureaucratese but it is not as complicated as it sounds:

---

Oscar turned 65 on June 15, 1993. Being a well informed senior, he knew he could apply for Part B on March 1, 1993 (March being three months before June, the month of his birth). He signed up on March 1. When his birthday arrived and he became officially eligible for Medicare, he was already signed up as part of the system and suffered no delay in receiving his benefits.

Unfortunately, Oscar's twin brother, Otto, was less informed. He did not get around to applying until October 10, 1993. Otto soon discovered that it was too late. He had waited too long to sign up for benefits as his initial enrollment period only lasted until September 30, 1993 (that date being three months after the end of June, the month of his birth).

---

The *"general enrollment period."* If you don't apply during the initial enrollment period, you can sign up once each year between January 1 and March 31, during the Medicare general enrollment period of every year. If you sign up during the general enrollment period, you will not be covered until July 1 of that year.

---

Because Otto had to wait until the general enrollment period before applying for Medicare, his benefits did not begin until July 1, 1994. On June 15, both Oscar and Otto enjoyed too much birthday cake and ended up seeing their doctors for severe stomach ache. Because Oscar had applied during the initial enrollment period, his doctor bills were covered by Medicare. Otto's were not.

---

In addition to missing coverage, you can be charged a ten percent per year add-on penalty to your Part B premium for each year you delay in applying for coverage. As you can see, failing to apply in a timely manner can be dangerous to your financial health. Thus, it is a good idea to apply for Medicare when you are first eligible.

If you are covered by a large group health insurance plan you receive as a benefit of employment, you may be able to delay enrollment in Medicare without paying a premium penalty and without waiting for a general enrollment period. To qualify for the special rule, you must enroll within seven months of the end of your employment or group health insurance coverage, or, if the plan is no longer classifiable as a large group health plan (one that covers 100 or more employees). For more details about this special enrollment period, contact your local Social Security office.

## IS THERE AN ALTERNATIVE TO MEDICARE?

As we will detail in Chapters 2 and 3, Medicare does not cover all medical expenses. For example, it will not usually pay for prescription medications, nor will it pay for a large part of the cost of your first day of covered hospitalization. Because of this, your yearly health care expenses can be substantial, even if you are covered by Medicare.

For this reason, many seniors supplement Medicare by purchasing a private health insurance, called Medigap insurance (see Chapter 4). But Medigap insurance can cost a lot of money. Thus, many seniors would like an alternative that will provide broad coverage without the extra out-of-pocket expenses that exist under Medicare.

That alternative is a health maintenance organization, known as an HMO. An HMO is a medical insurance plan that allows you to receive all of your covered health care for little or no cost. In an HMO, doctor's visits may cost nothing or only a few dollars, prescription expenses may be paid, and all hospitalizations may come at no charge to you. Moreover, preventive care is covered, which is usually not the case with regular Medicare benefits.

You may be saying, "This sounds too good to be true. What's the catch?" That's a very important question, for as a wise man once said, "There's no such thing as a free lunch." Here is the catch: Medicare is "fee for service" health insurance. That is, you are free to select your own doctor and you may be admitted into most hospitals. On the other hand, in an HMO, you give up this freedom of choice. You can only use the doctors who are approved by the HMO and you must use HMO approved hospitals and other medical facilities, or you receive no benefits. This means you may have to give up your own doctor and may not be able to be hospitalized in the facility nearest your home. There are usually two exceptions to this rule: If you seek emergency (which usually means life-or-death) medical treatment at a non-plan-approved hospital emergency room, or you require medical treatment when you are outside the geographical area covered by the HMO. Ask your HMO for details.

There is something else you need to know about the HMO option. Once enrolled in the HMO, *you lose your standard Medicare benefits.* That means that any treatment you seek outside your HMO will not be covered by Medicare, just as it will not be covered by your HMO. In such a case the full cost of your health care would have to be paid out of your own pocket.

---

The twin brothers Oscar and Otto both loved strawberries but were allergic. One day, after eating strawberries, both began to scratch and scratch. Oscar was on Medicare and was able to go to his neighborhood hospital emergency room and receive immediate treatment. Otto, on the other hand, had decided to use Medicare to join an HMO. He went to the same hospital as Oscar but when the hospital found out he was not on Medicare and determined it was not a life or death emergency, they directed him to the HMO hospital which was more than 30 miles away. Oscar had to pay for a portion of his treatment but received immediate help. Otto's treatment was delayed by two hours but he had to pay nothing for his treatment. Both felt they had made the right choice.

---

There is no "right" and "wrong" in choosing to stay with Medicare or to go with an HMO. With an HMO:

- You will probably pay less for health care and medical prescriptions.
- You give up your freedom of choice to choose your own doctor.
- You must get special permission from your personal doctor to go to a physician who is a specialist (i.e., a cardiologist, a psychiatrist, an orthopedic surgeon, etc.).
- You will not be covered by HMO benefits throughout the country and will have to learn the HMO's payment rules regarding medical care you receive out of your area of HMO coverage.

On the other hand, by staying with the Medicare program:

- You will probably pay more for your overall health care.
- You are covered throughout the nation.
- You can choose any doctor you want who is a participating physician with Medicare, including a specialist.

If you decide to go the HMO route, remember the following:

- Make sure the HMO is approved by Medicare. Medicare will only pay for your membership in HMOs that are so approved.
- You are no longer a part of the Medicare system in most circumstances. Instead, your rights are limited to those you receive as an HMO member. Be sure you understand them.
- The quality of HMOs vary greatly, so be sure to shop around before you sign up.
- Make sure your HMO is financially sound. There have been a rash of HMO bankruptcies in recent years. Contact your State Department of Corporations to inquire into the financial health of the HMO, or ask your insurance agent about this important issue.

If you find you don't like the HMO concept, you can change your mind and "disenroll" and get your standard Medicare benefits restored. The HMO must assist you in disenrolling and must notify Medicare. If you choose to disenroll, be sure to instruct the HMO to give you a *written* explanation of the process, including a notification of the time it takes to leave the HMO and again be eligible for standard Medicare benefits.

## WHAT IF WORK COVERS MY INSURANCE?

Not everyone retires at age 65: just ask George Burns. Many of these working seniors, like their younger counterparts, are covered by group health insurance as an employee benefit. Under federal law, group health plans must offer the same insurance benefits to older workers as they do to other employees.

If you have health insurance through work, you are still eligible to join Medicare upon reaching your 65th birthday, since Medicare eligibility is not based on the level of your income or upon your retirement. If you sign up, and your employer has 20 or more employees and you are covered by group health insurance through work, Medicare becomes a secondary payer of your medical bills and those of your spouse, age 65 or over. That means that your health insurance company must make *first* payment for medical services you receive, and not Medicare. However, Medicare may be obliged to pick up part or all of the tab for what your private health insurance doesn't cover, depending on the individual circumstances.

There are other conditions when Medicare may serve only as a back-up plan to other insurance policies. For example, if you are injured in an auto accident, Medicare may only pay what your auto insurance company doesn't cover. Or if injured on the job, Medicare may only pay what your workers' compensation claims don't pick up.

Medicare is relatively inexpensive to purchase if you qualify for free Part A coverage. That being so, if you are 65, it is probably a good idea to sign up for the program even if you have other health insurance, so as to give yourself the added protection of Medicare as back-up coverage.

## WHAT IF I'M OUT OF THE COUNTRY?

Many seniors love to spend their retirement years seeing the world. That is all well and good, but be aware that except under very limited circumstances, you won't be covered by Medicare when you are out of the country. If you are planning to travel, you may wish to buy travel insurance or discuss with the Consulate of the countries you will visit whether their health care system will protect you if you are sick or injured. (Unlike the United States, most industrialized nations have comprehensive national health insurance, which often protects visitors.) Also, Medigap health insurance policies may provide protection if you travel (see Chapter 4).

Now that we have completed our overview, let's turn to the nuts and bolts of Medicare coverage. We will begin with hospitalization coverage and other benefits that are provided under Medicare, Part A.

# 2

# MEDICARE, PART A

Hospitals can charge hundreds or even thousands of dollars a day. Woe unto the person who is hospitalized without insurance, which is the primary reason that Part A is so important to your financial security.

Part A covers four basic health care services: inpatient (admitted to the hospital) services, inpatient care in a skilled nursing facility following a hospital stay, home health and *hospice care*. It may also pay for blood transfusions. We will discuss these one at a time.

## HOSPITALIZATION BENEFITS

Let's look first at the hospitalization benefits available to you under Part A. The rules of coverage and benefit payments can be quite strict, and it is important that you fully understand the topic so that you can fully benefit from the law. The discussion will at times be quite detailed. For that reason, we will follow a question and answer format.

## When Are Hospitalizations Covered by Medicare?

Part A Medicare will only pay benefits if your hospitalization is considered "medically and reasonably necessary." In order to be considered medically and reasonably necessary, your treatment must meet *all* of the following four conditions:

- A state licensed doctor has prescribed inpatient hospital care for you.
- You require the kind of care provided only in a hospital.
- The hospital participates in the Medicare program. (Most, but not all, hospitals do. In certain emergency situations, Medicare will pick up the cost of emergency treatment if the hospital does not participate in Medicare.)
- The Medicare oversight board (called a Peer Review Organization) does not disapprove your stay. Thus, if your doctor seeks to admit you to the hospital but the peer review board determines that your care could be handled on an outpatient (nonhospitalized) basis, the Medicare payment for the treatment will not be approved. (This will rarely be an issue since your doctor and the hospital will know the kinds of maladies that will not be approved for in-the-hospital care.)

> Oscar was suffering from an abdominal pain. His physician, Dr. Playit Safe, decided to hospitalize Oscar for a few days of tests. The review board in the hospital, in reviewing the records, decided that the tests could be performed without admitting Oscar into the hospital. Thus, Part A would not cover the costs of hospitalization. Oscar had to decide whether to pay for the stay in the hospital himself or to have his medical care delivered in a way that would be covered by Medicare.

As illustrated by the above example, it is important to remember that Medicare does not decide whether or not you can receive the treatment prescribed. It only determines whether or not Medicare health insurance will *pay the tab* for the treatment. Of course, in the real world, if Medicare won't cover it, most, or many people can't afford the treatment.

## What Services Does Medicare Pay For?

If Medicare approves of your hospitalization, the following services are paid for by Medicare, subject to *deductibles* and *copayments* you owe (see below):

- A semiprivate room (two to four beds in a room)
- All your meals, including special diets
- Regular nursing services
- Costs of special care units, such as intensive care (so long as they are reasonably and medically necessary)
- Drugs furnished by the hospital during your hospital stay
- Blood transfusions furnished by the hospital during your stay
- Lab tests included in your hospital bill
- Radiological services such as X-rays
- Medical supplies, such as casts and bandages
- Use of appliances, such as a wheelchair
- Operating and recovery room costs
- Rehabilitation services, such as physical therapy and occupational therapy

Charges for personal convenience items that the hospital provides, such as for a television or telephone, are paid by you.

## HOW BENEFITS ARE CALCULATED

There are three different concepts to keep in mind when calculating your Medicare hospitalization benefits – the amount of time you spend in the hospital that Medicare will pay for, the proportion of the bill that Medicare pays, and the amount of the bill you must pay.

## The Issue of Time

It is important to understand how long your hospitalization will be covered by Medicare. Medicare defines both how long you will be covered and the amount of your bill that the government will pay, by breaking your stay in the hospital down into lengths of time called *benefit periods*. A benefit period is a way of measuring your use of services. The benefit period begins on the day you are admitted to the hospital. It ends when you have been out of the hospital or other facility primarily providing skilled care (such as a skilled nursing care facility) for 60 consecutive days, including the day of discharge.

Why is this important? Because the extent and amount of your coverage depends on *the time you spend in the hospital* or other covered care facility during each benefit period. If you do not stay out of the hospital long enough to end a benefit period (longer than 60 days), your rehospitalization could be treated by Medicare as if you had never left the hospital in the first place. Thus, if you were hospitalized for 30 days, released for 10 days and placed back in the hospital for another 15 days, Medicare could treat your hospitalization as a single 45-day hospital stay. This can cost you extra money because when you are hospitalized for a long period of time you can be forced to pay a greater share of the cost of your care. On the other hand, if you get past the 60 days and must be hospitalized again, you can be forced to pay another deductible.

## The Deductible

Like many insurance plans, Medicare Part A hospitalization coverage has a deductible. That means you must pay a specified amount of money out of your pocket before Medicare pays any benefits. In 1993, the deductible was $676 for each benefit period. The amount of the Part A deductible tends to be raised by Congress every year.

Oscar was hospitalized for surgery. Oscar paid the $676 deductible. Twenty days later he was discharged. Five days after his discharge, complications set in, causing a rehospitalization. Because the benefit period had not lapsed, he did not have to pay another deductible.

Oscar's twin brother Otto, also had surgery. He too paid the $676 deductible and was hospitalized for twenty days. After discharge, Otto remained healthy for 75 days and then the doctor discovered that Otto had not healed properly. Otto was readmitted for treatment to correct the problem. He had to pay a second deductible because his benefit period had lapsed.

## Copayments

The amount of your hospital bill that Medicare pays for and the amount you must pay depends upon the amount of time you are hospitalized. In 1993, the formula was as follows:

- Day 1–60: Medicare pays 100 percent of covered hospitalization services, after you have paid the deductible. (This does not include the payment of your doctor. That expense is paid under Part B; see Chapter 3.)
- Day 61–90: You pay the first $169 per day (known as the copayment) and Medicare pays the balance.
- Day 91–Discharge: You are completely responsible for the charge, unless you use "reserve days" (see below).

In 1993, Otto was admitted to the hospital after slipping in the bath tub and severely injuring his back. His recovery was slow but he was able to be discharged after 45 days. Ten days later, he was readmitted for 30 more days. His out-of-pocket costs were $3,211, consisting of:
- The $676 deductible; and
- $2,535 copayments (about $169 per day for 15 days – day 61-75 of total days of hospitalization. There was not a second deductible owed because less than 60 days had passed from Otto's initial discharge.)

### Reserve Days

Thankfully, most hospitalizations do not require more than 90 days. However, seriously ill or injured patients do sometimes require such extended care. For this reason, Medicare has "reserve days" of coverage that you can use any time the length of your hospitalization exhausts the 90-day basic coverage period. You need to know the following about reserve days:

- You have a total of 60 reserve days in your lifetime. Once the 60 days have been used, they are gone forever.
- Reserve days are not renewable. This is in direct contrast for days 1–90, Part A Hospitalization coverage, which is renewable with every new benefit period.
- You must pay a copayment when you use a reserve day. In 1993, the amount of this copayment was $338 per day.
- If you are hospitalized for more than 90 days and do not want to use your reserve days, you must inform the hospital in writing. The hospital will assume you are using reserve days unless you tell them otherwise in writing. If you choose not to use a reserve day, you are responsible for the total cost of your hospital care. (Of course, you may have insurance to help pay for these services; see Chapter 4.)

## YOUR LENGTH OF STAY

As if all of this weren't enough to have to understand, there's another little complication that we have to discuss. It is called the *Diagnosis Related Group* (DRG) System. Its purpose is to cut Medicare's cost to the government. Its effect may cause you to be discharged from the hospital earlier than would be the case if you were not having your treatment paid for by Medicare.

Here's how the DRG system works:

## The Diagnosis

The length of your stay in the hospital does not control how much the hospital receives as payment for your care from Medicare. Rather, your diagnosis controls how much Medicare will pay the hospital based on a predetermined schedule of benefits. The following example reveals why many doctors and patients complain that Medicare patients are being discharged "sooner and sicker," as a result of this policy.

> Otto was diagnosed with the dreaded foot-in-mouth disease. Under the DRG system, a determination has been made by Medicare after studying the issue that the average hospitalization required to treat foot-in-mouth disease is five days. Thus, the hospital was paid five days' worth of hospital care from Medicare for Otto's hospitalization, regardless of the actual length of his stay.

If Otto's stay was three days, the hospital made a big profit. If it was five days, the hospital still made a profit, since profit is built into the system. However, if Otto's treatment required 10 days, the hospital would lose money on Otto's care. Thus, the financial incentive created by the DRG system is obvious: release the patient from the hospital as soon as possible.

## How Your Hospital Can Pressure You to Leave

Under the law, you cannot be forced to leave the hospital before it is medically safe to do so. However, if your hospital believes that your continued hospitalization is no longer medically reasonable or necessary, they will send you a document known as a *Notice of Noncoverage*. The effect of this notice is to tell you that after the date of proposed noncoverage, the hospital expects you to pay the entire bill for your hospitalized care. That, of course, creates a strong financial incentive for you to leave the hospital.

*Note:* The hospital cannot begin to charge you for your own care unless it provides you with a written Notice of Noncoverage before terminating Medicare benefits.

### Appealing the Notice of Noncoverage

If you do not agree with the hospital, you can appeal to a group of doctors paid to review Medicare cases, called the Peer Review Organization (PRO). This is an important right, and you should exercise it in your own behalf if you believe that a mistake is being made.

Here's how the process works:

**If the Notice of Noncoverage states that your physician agrees with the hospital's decision:**

- You must make your telephone or written request to the PRO by noon of the first work day after you receive the Notice. (The telephone number and address of the PRO for your hospital can be found in a written document called "An Important Message From Medicare," which you will receive from the hospital upon your admission.)
- The PRO must ask you your views before making its decision.
- Based on the records and your communication, the PRO will make their decision. You will be notified of the decision by telephone or mail.
- If the PRO agrees with the hospital, you can be charged for your hospital stay beginning at noon of the day after you receive the PRO decision.
- You are not responsible for the cost of your stay before you receive the PRO decision.

**If the Notice of Noncoverage states that the PRO agrees with the hospital's decision:**

- You should make your request for reconsideration immediately upon receiving the Notice.

- The PRO can take up to three working days from receipt of your request to complete the review.
- Since the PRO has already reviewed your case (probably because your doctor and the hospital disagreed and the hospital brought the matter before the PRO), the hospital is permitted to begin billing you for the cost of your stay beginning with the third calendar day after you receive your Notice of Noncoverage.

Thus, if you stay in the hospital pending the outcome of your appeal, and you lose the appeal, you may be compelled to pay for one or more days of your hospitalization yourself.

### Appealing the Decision of the PRO

If you lose at the PRO stage and wish to continue the legal fight, you are legally entitled to do so. Contact your local legal services office for seniors for help (see Appendix 7).

All of this can be quite complicated but it is very important for you to understand. If you have any questions, ask the hospital's patient liaison to assist you.

## SKILLED NURSING FACILITY CARE

Often, people are discharged from a hospital but are not yet medically ready to return to their homes. Under such conditions, they may be admitted for further recuperation in a convalescent center known as a skilled nursing facility. For purposes of Medicare, a skilled nursing facility is one that provides skilled nursing or skilled rehabilitation and related health services, care that can only be performed by, or under the supervision of, licensed nursing personnel.

Medicare will only pay for your care in a skilled nursing facility under limited conditions. First, the treatment cannot be *custodial care*. Care is considered custodial if it can be provided by workers who do not have professional training or skills and it is provided to help you meet your personal needs. Activities such as bathing, assistance with meals and directing the taking of prescription medication, are generally considered custodial. Most long-term nursing home care is considered custodial and therefore is not covered by Medicare.

Second, in order for your treatment in a skilled nursing facility to be covered by Part A, it must meet all of the following requirements:

- Your condition requires daily skilled nursing or re-habilitation services, which as a practical matter, can only be provided in a skilled nursing facility.
- You must have been in a hospital *three days in a row* (not including your day of discharge) before you are admitted to the skilled care facility. (If you leave the skilled nursing home but are readmitted to it within 30 days, you do not need a new three-day hospital stay to qualify for care.)
- You are admitted within a short time (generally within 30 days) after you leave the hospital.
- You are treated in the skilled nursing facility for the same illness as in the hospital or for a condition that arose in the nursing facility while you were treated.
- A medical professional certifies that you need the services on a daily basis.
- The "Medicare Intermediary" does not disapprove of the stay. (The intermediary is to a skilled nursing facility what a PRO is to a hospital.)

Coverage for treatment in a skilled nursing facility is minimal with a maximum of 100 days total coverage in each benefit period. There is no deductible and the patient does not have to pay for covered services for the first 20 days. From day 21 through 100 a copayment is required that was $84.50 per day in 1993. (*Note:* Your doctor's bill is covered under Part B, not Part A.) You can appeal Medicare's decision not to pay for your nursing care to the Medicare Intermediary. If you disagree with the Interme-diary's initial decision, you can bring further appeals through Social Security. Contact your local office for more details.

> Oscar was hospitalized for five days after a fall and then, on the advice of his doctor, was released into a nursing facility, where he received assistance with hygiene, eating and toilet. After 30 days, he felt well enough to go home. Medicare did not pay for the services because they did not involve skilled nursing but rather, custodial care.
>
> In 1993, his brother Otto, was also hospitalized for five days after he suffered a stroke. Otto's doctor prescribed treatment in a nursing facility, where he received physical therapy to restore strength to his right arm, and speech therapy to help restore his ability to communicate. He was released after 40 days. Medicare covered part of the cost of nursing facility. Otto had to pay the balance of $1,690. (The first 20 days were free, the second 20 days cost Otto $84.50 per day for a total of $1,690.)

## HOME HEALTH CARE

As the costs of hospitalization increases, home health care is being turned to with increasing frequency to cut costs while providing necessary care. It is also now considered an alternative to hospitalization. Medicare Part A covers such skilled medical services provided in your home and there is no limit on the days of covered care Medicare will pay.

Medicare has established the following specific conditions that must be met before Medicare will pay for medical services provided in your home:

- The care must include periodically provided skilled nursing care (such as changing surgical dressings, or giving injections, physical therapy or speech therapy).
- You must be homebound.
- You are under the care of a physician who determines you need home health care.
- Your doctor sets up a home health care plan for you.
- The home health care agency participates in Medicare.

People who need help with housework, cooking or other matters of personal living (custodial care) do not qualify for Medicare benefits. Nor is twenty-four hour nursing care provided.

After a small deductible, Medicare pays the full approved cost of all covered home health care visits. You may be charged only for those services that Medicare does not cover. Medicare pays for 80 percent of the cost of durable medical equipment (wheelchairs, hospital beds, etc.). You are responsible for the other 20 percent. The home health care agency will submit bills to Medicare directly.

## HOSPICE CARE

Hospice care is designed to treat the terminally ill, not to prolong life or bring about a cure, but to maintain the quality of life through pain control, symptom management and support services. Hospice care can include care in a hospice facility or in the home.

Three conditions must be met for Medicare Part A to pick up the cost of hospice care:

- Your doctor must certify that you are terminally ill.
- You elect to receive hospice treatment instead of standard Medicare benefits.
- Your care is provided by a Medicare participating hospice service provider.

Part A covers a broader range of services and products in its hospice provisions than will be found in other areas of either Part A or Part B coverage. For example, doctor's services are paid for without the necessity of a copayment (see Chapter 3), as are the cost of prescription drugs for pain relief and symptom management, expenses usually not paid for by Medicare. Medical social services are covered, as is personal counseling, homemaker services and respite care which allows care-giving family members some time off from the intense task of helping a loved one navigate the transition between life and death.

You can leave hospice care and elect to return to the general Medicare system, which would make you again eligible for Medicare payment of treatment designed to save your life. However, if you do leave the hospice program, pain medication and other such hospice-related treatment may not be covered.

There are no deductibles for hospice care. In 1993, the patient was responsible for five percent of the cost of out-patient drugs or $5 toward that cost, whichever was *less*. That can save a lot of money! For inpatient hospice care, the patient paid five percent of the Medicare allowed rate, something under $5 per day.

If during the hospice care, the patient requires treatment for a condition not related to the terminal illness, all other Medicare rates and benefits apply.

## BLOOD

Both Parts A and B have blood benefits. They are detailed in the summary charts set forth in Appendices 1 and 2.

Part A is vital to your health and financial well-being. Paying for hospitalization and skilled nursing services only partially protects your health and your pocketbook. You also need coverage for services such as your doctor's care and laboratory tests. That's where Part B comes in, which is the subject of the next chapter.

*3*

# MEDICARE, PART B

In addition to hospitalization and associated Part A coverages, Medicare has created a program to help you pay for other medical expenses, such as doctors' bills and diagnostic testing. This is a very important part of Medicare. Most medical services are provided in doctors' offices, clinics and diagnostic testing centers rather than in an inpatient hospital setting, and thus are not covered by Part A. Even when you are hospitalized, you still need Part B to pay for your doctor's services. For example, if you have surgery, Part A will pay for the hospitalization, but Part B will pay for the surgeon and anesthetist. It is vital that you understand what is and what is not covered by Part B Medicare. Otherwise, you could find that Medicare refuses to pay for your medical care or that you have to pay more for your health care than you expected. For example, some doctors charge more than Medicare will pay for services. Other doctors do not. Choosing a doctor who accepts Medicare's determination can save you a lot of money. (See the discussion, "Accepting the Assignment," later in this chapter.)

## UNDERSTANDING PART B BENEFITS

Now, let's turn to a discussion of the health care services that are covered under Part B, those that are not, and how you tell the difference.

### What Services Are Covered by Part B?

Part B covers the following areas of health care:

- Doctors' services
- Outpatient hospital care
- Diagnostic tests
- Durable medical equipment (wheelchairs, respirators, etc.)
- Ambulance services
- Administered drugs
- Immunosuppressive drugs for one year after discharge from the hospital after an organ transplant
- Prosthetic devices, such as colostomy bags and corrective lenses needed after a cataract operation
- The services of some health care professionals who are not doctors, such as physical therapists and speech pathologists
- Medical supplies, such as splints, dressings and casts
- Chiropractors in very limited circumstances
- Second opinion before surgery
- Oral surgery in limited circumstances, so long as it is not deemed by Medicare to be "dental care"
- Miscellaneous coverages, such as kidney dialysis

### What Areas Are Not Covered by Part B?

It is almost as important to know what areas of your health care Medicare will not pay for as it is to understand the areas that Medicare covers. These non-covered services are called exclusions. Medicare's Part B exclusions include the following:

- Routine physicals. As a general rule, Medicare does not pay for preventive care, such as routine medical examinations. (There are limited exceptions, such as mammograms and Pap smears.) This is unfortunate, since the sooner a malady is discovered, usually the less expensive it is to treat and more likely to cure.
- Most routine foot care and dental care. This can be rough on seniors who may need dentures or the services of a podiatrist.
- Examinations for prescribing eyeglasses or hearing aids.
- Most immunizations. However, flu shots are generally covered, as are injections to prevent specific infections or which may be required after receiving an injury.
- Cosmetic surgery, unless it is needed because of accidental injury, or to improve the function of a malformed part of the body.
- Most prescription drugs. If you take your own medicine at home, even if you inject it into your own veins, the cost of your medicine is not covered. (Some doctors give free samples to help seniors cope with the cost of medicine.)

---

Otto went to his doctor for his annual physical. The doctor checked him from head-to-toe, and gave him a clean bill of health. Otto applied for Medicare benefits and was turned down on the basis that the examination was routine and not due to the existence of physical symptoms.

Oscar followed Otto into the doctor's office, complaining of acid indigestion and dizziness. The doctor gave him a complete physical, which found nothing wrong. However, unlike Otto's experience, the cost of Oscar's examination was covered by Medicare simply because the doctor was searching for an illness.

---

### What Is My Share of the Bill?

Like any insurance policy, Medicare contains some "fine print" that you need to understand if you are to minimize your share of the cost of your covered medical care. Here are some issues to consider when planning financially for your medical treatment:

**The Deductible.** Before Medicare pays one cent, you must pay the first $100 (in 1993) of your Part B covered care. That amount rises each, year as the government seeks to control Medicare costs. However, the good news is that unlike Part A, there is only one deductible for the whole year. You do not have to meet separate deductibles for each kind of covered service.

**Copayments.** Medicare Part B does not pay for 100 percent of the cost of your treatment. Like many private insurance health plans, it pays 80 percent and you pay 20 percent.

**The "Reasonable Charge."** Medicare does *not* pay for 80 percent of the *actual charge* made by your doctor, but rather, it will pay what Medicare considers to be a "reasonable charge." Let's say your doctor treats you for a bacterial infection. Her charge is $450. If Medicare considers the reasonable charge to be $300, it will pay 80 percent of $300, not 80 percent of $450.

**"Accepting the Assignment."** Few if any doctors charge lower than Medicare's reasonable charge. However, as we noted earlier, some will accept Medicare's reasonable charge as the amount they will bill for services and others will not. Those doctors that do are called doctors who will "accept the assignment." That is a distinction with a definite difference, a difference that can cost you a lot of money.

When your doctor accepts the Medicare assignment, he or she agrees to accept payment directly from Medicare. This means you don't have to pay the doctor and then wait for Medicare to reimburse you. Of course, you will still have a financial responsibility to your doctor, for the deductible, if owed, and the 20 percent copayment.

Most importantly, if you go to a doctor who accepts the assignment, you will pay less money. The reason? A doctor who agrees to accept the assignment also agrees to accept the Medicare reasonable charge as the full amount of the fee for the medical treatment.

On the other hand, a doctor who does not accept the assignment is free to charge whatever the market will bear for your treatment. Also, if your doctor does not accept the assignment, he or she can demand full payment from you at the time services are rendered and you must wait to be reimbursed from Medicare.

There's more. If your doctor refuses to accept the assignment, Medicare will still only pay 80 percent of the reasonable charge. This means that you must pay the 20 percent copayment *and* the difference between the actual fee and Medicare's reasonable charge. In some cases, that difference amounts to a lot of money.

---

Otto went to his doctor for treatment of a kidney ailment. The total charge made by the doctor was $1,000. Otto's doctor did not accept the assignment. Otto paid the doctor $1,000. Later, Medicare determined that the reasonable charge for the care was $800. It then repaid Otto $640 (80 percent of $800). Thus, Otto paid $360 out of his own pocket (20 percent of $800 plus the $200 difference between the doctor's actual charge and the reasonable charge as determined by Medicare).

On the same day, Otto's twin, Oscar, sought treatment for an identical ailment. Like Otto's doctor, the actual charge for the treatment was $1,000. However, Oscar had chosen a doctor who accepted the assignment. After the treatment, Oscar did not have to write his doctor a check for $1,000 because the doctor would be paid directly from Medicare. Medicare again determined that the reasonable charge for the treatment was $800. It then paid Oscar's doctor $640. Oscar, in turn, paid the doctor his 20 percent copayment of $160, which was deemed payment in full. Thus, by choosing a doctor who accepted the assignment, Oscar paid $200 less than his brother for the same treatment, given on the same day for the same ailment, and having been charged the same fee.

---

If you can't find a doctor who accepts the assignment in your area, contact your local Social Security office. They will have a list of doctors who do.

**The Treatment Must Be Considered "Medically Necessary."** Cost containment has become the order-of-the-day in Medicare. One way the government saves money is by having Medicare reserve the right to judge whether your health care service was actually "medically necessary." If it is determined by the oversight people, known under Part

B as "Carrier," that the treatment was not medically necessary, it will pay no benefits and you will have to pay the bill yourself. (You can appeal the decision. The appeal process is similar to appealing decisions regarding Social Security, although relatively few appeals are successful. See Chapter 8 and contact your local Social Security office.)

Most doctors have a great deal of experience with this issue and will tell you in advance if there may be a problem with Medicare. You can also contact your Carrier in advance of your treatment to ensure that Medicare will pay its share of the bill. The address and telephone numbers of the Medicare Carriers can be found in Appendix 6.

### What Other Services Are Covered?

As summarized at the beginning of this chapter, Part B pays for part or all of many medical services other than those rendered by your doctor. Here are some examples:

**Outpatient Hospital Services.** Often patients receive services in a hospital on an outpatient basis. For example, if you cut your finger badly enough to need stitches, you may need to go to an emergency room, where you will receive care and then be sent home. Or, you may go to a hospital for a day of diagnostic tests and return home when that ordeal is complete.

Unlike inpatient hospitalization, you must pay 20 percent of the hospital's charge (after the yearly deductible has been met) for outpatient services, while Medicare pays 80 percent. Remember, this charge is in addition to your doctor's bill or other medical professionals who may charge separately for their services, such as a radiologist.

---

**Outpatient Hospital Services
Covered By Part B**

• Services in an emergency room or outpatient clinic, including same-day surgery (where you check into the hospital, have surgery and then check out)

• Laboratory tests billed by the hospital

• Mental health care in a partial hospitalization psychiatric program

• X-rays and other radiology services billed by the hospital

• Medical supplies, such as a cast put on in an emergency room

• Blood transfusions furnished to you as an outpatient

---

**Home Health Care.** If you have Part A, that section pays for home health care. If you are not covered by Part A, Part B pays the same benefits as Part A for home health care.

**Outpatient Therapies.** If you suffer from a debilitating illness or injury that requires physical therapy, occupational therapy or speech therapy, Medicare Part B will pay benefits if you are an outpatient. Your doctor's participation is key to Medicare paying for your treatment. In order for your therapy to be covered, *all* of the following three conditions must be met:

• Your doctor must prescribe the service.
• Your doctor or therapist must set up the plan of treatment.
• Your doctor must periodically review the plan.

The treatment can be provided in your own home by a Medicare-participating home health care agency, in a skilled nursing facility, participating hospital, rehabilitation agency or a public health agency.

The 80/20 percent rule applies to outpatient treatment. Only approved charges will be covered by Medicare. Any services Medicare will not pay are your responsibility.

Also, you should be aware that Medicare will pay your therapist a *maximum payment of* $750 per year (in 1993).

**Independent Laboratory Services.** Most of us have had the experience of going to a laboratory at the direction of a doctor, having tests, and then waiting and waiting for the results. While Medicare cannot speed up the delivery of your test results, it will help pay the bill. Moreover, Medicare will pay the full approved fee for covered clinical diagnostic tests, if the laboratory has been approved by Medicare to perform them. The lab must accept the assignment for the tests and cannot bill you for them. Neither can your doctor.

Not every laboratory is approved by Medicare and some labs are only approved for a limited number of procedures. Before going to a laboratory for prescribed testing, make sure it is on Medicare's approved list. If in doubt, ask your doctor. If your doctor does not know whether the lab is approved, contact your local Medicare Carrier (see Appendix 6). Remember, if you go to an unapproved lab, you will have to pay the costs of the tests yourself, so be sure the lab is Medicare approved for the test you are being given.

Beyond understanding your Part B benefits, you should learn how to access them. Happily, claims processing is easy.

## HOW ARE CLAIMS FILED?

That is your doctor's responsibility. He or she is required to file Medicare claims on your behalf, whether or not they accept the assignment. These claims must be submitted within one year or they face financial penalties. If your doctor refuses to perform this service, contact your Medicare carrier.

There may be limited circumstances in which you will have to file your own claim. If in doubt, contact your carrier. If a person entitled to Medicare benefits has died, the beneficiaries or administrator of the *estate* should contact the carrier for further instructions on filing a claim or obtaining legally-owed Medicare reimbursement.

## How Do I Find Out What Benefits Have Been Paid?

When a claim on your behalf is filed with Medicare, you are entitled under the law to an explanation of the benefits paid or refused. This notice is called the *Explanation of Your Medicare Part B Benefits.* The notice will tell you what services were covered, what charges were approved as reasonable, how much was credited toward your $100 annual deductible and the amount Medicare paid on the claim. If Medicare refuses to pay your claim, which rarely happens for treatment of actual ailments, or if Medicare sets a reasonable charge you believe is too low, or if you believe any other error has been made, contact your local Carrier.

Each region of the company has a Carrier. If you have any questions about the coverage details as they relate to your individual circumstances, contact your Carrier. A complete list of Carriers can be found in Appendix 6. A chart-summary of Part B coverages can be found in Appendix 2.

Now, let's turn to the important issue of how you can supplement your Medicare coverage with privately purchased health insurance. These policies are known as Medigap policies. Understanding what these health insurance policies cover – and what they don't – can help you pick the right policy and save you a lot of money and aggravation.

# 4

# MEDIGAP INSURANCE

If you have read the last two chapters, you now know that your health care can cost you a lot of money, even if you have Medicare. For that reason, there is a thriving market in private health insurance policies for senior citizens designed to supplement Medicare benefits. These polices are called Medigap insurance.

Over the years, there has been a great deal of confusion about Medigap insurance. Some unscrupulous carriers have tried to get business by implying that they are an arm of the government. This is not true! *The government does not sell any Medigap policies.* All Medigap insurance is sold by private-sector businesses. Moreover, some seniors mistakenly believed, or were led to believe by unscrupulous sales people, that Medigap insurance covers everything that Medicare does not pay for. This too is mistaken. Some seniors have also made the expensive mistake of buying more than one Medigap policy. Unfortunately, that was money washed down the drain.

Problems in the industry got so bad that the federal government was forced to step in and establish uniformity among the policies that can be sold in the marketplace. The Medigap insurance industry is now only allowed to market 10 standardized policies. This chapter explains the diff-

erences among the policies, and gives you the information
you need to know to make an intelligent decision on
whether to buy Medigap insurance.

## PLUGGING THE GAPS IN MEDICARE COVERAGE

When Medicare does not pay for part or all of a health
care service, this is called a "gap" in coverage. There are
two distinct types of gaps: benefit gaps and coverage gaps.

A benefit gap is one where Medicare covers the type of
medical treatment you received but you must pay a
copayment or a deductible. For example, if your doctor
treats you for kidney stones, Medicare will pay 80 percent
of the reasonable charge of the treatment. The remaining
20 percent is your responsibility and constitutes the benefit
gap.

A coverage gap occurs where Medicare pays no benefits
at all for the medical care you received. For example, say
that you receive treatment for a skin condition and your
doctor prescribes an ointment for you to apply to your skin
at home. As you will recall from Chapters 2 and 3,
Medicare does not pay for prescription drugs or medicine,
thus you must pay for the ointment out of your own pocket.

The distinction between these two kinds of gaps is important. Medigap policies generally pay benefits *only for
benefit gaps.* It is the rare (and expensive) insurance policy
that will pay benefits where Medicare allows no coverage at
all. (Don't confuse Medigap insurance with nursing home
insurance. They are not the same at all. Nursing home
insurance policies will be discussed in Chapter 15.)

## COMPARING MEDIGAP POLICIES

If you decide you want to purchase Medigap insurance,
you should compare the different policies on the market in
your state to see which is best for your individual circumstances. Here are the areas to look for:

## Is the Part A Deductible Covered?

As you will recall, there is a significant deductible under Medicare Part A, a deductible that can be charged for each occurrence (see page 20). However, unless you are so gravely ill or injured that you require extended hospitalization or you elect to stay in the hospital after Medicare benefits cease, the deductible is probably the only charge you will be responsible to pay to the hospital out of your own pocket. So, any Medigap policy you purchase should cover the Part A deductible. Otherwise, it may be of little real benefit to you if you are hospitalized.

## Are Long-Term Hospitalizations Covered?

After the first 60 days, your hospitalization will begin to cost you a great deal of money (see page 21). One important area of policy comparison is the extent that the expensive daily copayments to the hospital are covered. For example, one Medigap policy might pay the entire copayment, while another might pay $200 a day, and still another might have no coverage at all.

## What About Skilled Nursing Home Copayments?

Your responsibility to pay for skilled nursing home care begins after you have been in the facility for 20 days. That's not a very long time if you are recovering from a serious ailment or injury or if you must remain in the facility because you don't have anyone to help care for you at home. A policy that does not help pay for skilled nursing home care copayments is not providing as much protection as you may need, especially since the DRG system Medicare uses to pay hospitals for your care encourages a speedy discharge. (See Chapter 2 for a discussion of the DRG system.)

## Is the Part B Deductible Covered?

This is of less pressing concern because the deductible is a relatively low amount – $100 per year in 1993 – and is only charged once per year, rather than per illness or occurrence.

## Is the Part B Twenty-Percent Copayment Covered?

This is of greater importance than the Part B deductible. As you will recall from the last chapter, you are obliged to pay 20 percent of the reasonable charge for medical services covered by Part B. That can add up to a lot of money over a year's time and Medicare patients often need help meeting their copayment responsibilities. Not all Medigap policies pay benefits for this obligation.

## Are Excess Charges Under Part B Covered?

Some doctors do not accept the assignment, and are thus not subject to Medicare cost containment procedures (see page 34). If you see such a doctor, you are responsible for the difference between the actual charge made by the doctor and the reasonable charge allowed by Medicare. (This is in addition to your 20 percent copayment responsibility.)

Many readers may be asking, who would use a doctor that refuses to accept the assignment? A doctor who is very popular may feel that he or she can avoid accepting the assignment. Many people go on Medicare and don't want to change doctors when they learn their current physician does not accept the assignment. Likewise, a specialist may not accept the assignment or a doctor may refuse to give you that financial break because he or she has little competition. Whatever the reason, if you choose or are forced to use a doctor who refuses to accept the assignment, this Medigap coverage can be very important to you.

## What Other Coverages Does the Policy Offer?

A few polices will pay for limited areas of coverage gaps, such as prescription benefits. If you can afford the monthly premium, you may be interested in this added protection.

## What Areas Aren't Covered by the Medigap Policy?

As with any insurance, there will be the proverbial fine print in your Medigap policy that will take away benefits you may think you have. For example, some Medigap policies have an exclusion that exempts preexisting health conditions from coverage for a period of time, usually six months. Or, a policy may have a ceiling which limits the amount of payments that will be made. Be sure you investigate all of the exclusions and conditions of coverage that limit benefits before you sign on the bottom line.

# THE STANDARDIZED MEDIGAP POLICIES

As mentioned, the federal government has required that Medigap policies be standardized to avoid confusion and prevent seniors from becoming victims of unsavory practices and fraud. Under the standardization plan, 10 different policies are allowed. One coverage contains only the minimum core benefit coverages (Plan A). The other nine include the core benefits package and then add differing combinations of extra coverage.

## Core Benefits Coverage

- Part A (Days 61–90)
- Lifetime reserve days (Days 91–150)
- An additional 365 days of hospitalization after all Medicare hospitalization benefits have been exhausted
- Coverage under Parts A and B for the reasonable cost of the first three pints of blood

- Coverage for the 20 percent copayment amount for Part B after the yearly deductible is met

The following chart outlines the other coverages that are available and highlights the differences among the 10 basic plans allowed to be sold in the United States. Plan A is the core benefits plan.

## Additional Benefits Coverage

| Additional Benefits:<br>PLANS: | A | B | C | D | E | F | G | H | I | J |
|---|---|---|---|---|---|---|---|---|---|---|
| Skilled Nursing Facility Consurance (Days 21–100) | | | X | X | X | X | X | X | X | X |
| Part A Deductible | | X | X | X | X | X | X | X | X | X |
| Part B Deductible | | | X | | | X | | | | X |
| Part B Excess Charge % Covered | | | | | | 100% | 80% | | 100% | 100% |
| Foreign Travel Emergency | | | X | X | X | X | X | X | X | X |
| At-Home Recovery | | | | X | | | X | | X | X |
| Prescription Drugs | | | | | | | | 1* | 1* | 2** |
| Preventive Medical Care | | | | | X | | | | | X |

1*   A BASIC BENEFIT WITH $250 ANNUAL DEDUCTIBLE, 50% COINSURANCE AND A $1,250 MAXIMUM ANNUAL BENEFIT (PLANS H AND I ABOVE)

2**   AN EXTENDED BENEFIT (PLAN J ABOVE) CONTAINING A $250 ANNUAL DEDUCTIBLE, 50% COINSURANCE AND A $3,000 MAXIMUM ANNUAL BENEFIT

(Source: 1993 Guide to Health Insurance for People with Medicare.)

Otto purchased the Core Policy (Plan A) to supplement his Medicare coverage. His twin brother Oscar purchased Plan D. Oscar paid $75 more per month in premiums. Both were in a serious auto accident while driving together to visit their mother. They landed in the hospital for 90 days and were then released. Both needed skilled nursing home care for 22 days after their release from the hospital.

Otto, who had paid less in Medigap insurance premiums, paid more for his Medicare-covered health care. He had to pay the Part A $676 deductible, while Oscar did not. Both received the same benefits for days 61-90 in the hospital, since that protection is part of the core benefits required of every Medigap policy. Medicare paid both Otto and Oscar's first 20 days in the skilled nursing facility. However, Otto had to pay for the final two days of his skilled nursing home care, while his brother received Medigap benefits for those days.

This illustration shows that Medigap insurance is like most kinds of insurance. The more protection you buy, the more money you pay for insurance. However, if you ever have to make a claim, the higher-priced policy is more likely to pay higher benefits.

## MEDICARE SELECT COVERAGE

There is a new form of Medicare supplemental insurance that is just entering the private marketplace. It is called Medicare SELECT. Medicare SELECT is supposed to charge a lower premium than traditional Medigap insurance. In return, you must agree to use health care professionals designated by the plan. The plan is not an HMO. It is more akin to a Preferred Provider Organization (PPO) that many private health insurers operate to cut premium costs. Unlike an HMO, SELECT will pay for the services of non-plan providers. However, if you go to a doctor who is not a designated provider, you will not receive full benefits. In an emergency, you can go to any physician or hospital and receive full benefits.

SELECT is a pilot program permitted by the government that will be evaluated in three years to see if it should be broadened to include the whole country. If the program does not continue after that time, participating companies will be required to provide for the continuation of Medigap coverage for those who have purchased SELECT policies. Fifteen states are expected to have these reduce-priced policies available. They are: AL, AZ, CA, FL, IN, KY, MO, MN, MI, ND, OH, OR, TX, WA, and WI.

## BUYING A POLICY

Purchasing any type of insurance takes knowledge and care. But when the policy is health insurance, the importance of your decision is magnified, because a wrong decision can cost so much money. Thus, when you shop for Medigap policies, be sure to take your time, compare policies and benefits, and remember the following:

### Use the "Free Look" Provisions

Insurance companies are required by law to give you at least 30 days to review your policy contract after you have purchased it. If you review the actual terms of the policy and you change your mind, you are entitled to cancel the policy and receive a refund. Be sure your company sends you the actual policy and then take the time to read it. If the policy is not what you want, exercise your rights to cancel it and find a better policy. (Be sure your new policy is in effect before your rejected policy lapses.)

### Don't Fall Prey to Hard Sell Tactics

It is unlawful for anyone selling Medigap insurance to use high-pressure sale tactics to force or frighten you into buying a policy, or to make misleading comparisons to get you to switch from one policy to another. It is also illegal to get information about your health care needs and then sell them to an insurance agent (called the "cold lead tactic"). In a cold lead, you are sent a postcard to fill out and mail back to the sender about your insurance needs. The card is then sold to an insurance agent who will, in turn, contact you to sell you a policy. If you have been the victim of hard sell or cold lead tactics, contact your state's insurance commissioner.

### Don't Buy Duplicate Coverage

Federal law now prohibits the sale of a Medicare supplemental policy to a person who already has another health insurance policy that provides coverage for *any* of the same benefits. This is called anti-duplicate protection. If anyone tries to get you to buy duplicate coverage, turn them in to your state insurance commissioner or Medicare so that law enforcement action can be taken against them.

### Don't Cancel Your Policy Until New Coverage Is Fully Effective

If you decide to change coverages, be sure to keep your old policy in full force and effect until all preexisting condition periods, waiting periods or other impediments to full coverage have expired.

### If in Doubt, Get Insurance Counseling

Many senior centers and other agencies that offer services to seniors provide counseling to answer your questions about Medigap policies. State insurance departments will also have educational materials available. National organizations, such as the American Association of Retired Persons (AARP), should also be able to help. Some even have telephone services to answer your questions. The addresses and telephone numbers of all state insurance departments are in Appendix 5 and the telephone numbers for those states offering telephone counseling services are in Appendix 9.

### Don't Buy a Policy If You're Eligible for Medicaid

If your income is near or under the poverty line, you may qualify for Medicaid, a government health care program designed to assist the poor. If you are qualified for Medicaid, you probably don't need to buy a Medigap policy, since Medicaid will cover much of what Medicare does not pay. If you do qualify for this health plan, save the money you would spend for Medigap premiums to pay for other necessities of life.

Medicaid is, in fact, the subject of the next chapter. Those of you who are concerned about paying for nursing home care should pay special attention, since Medicaid is the only government health care program that pays the cost of such facilities.

# 5

# MEDICAID

We now turn to Medicaid, the government health insurance program for the poor. Medicaid is an important program for any senior citizen or the family of a senior citizen, who may at some point in their lives have to be admitted into a nursing home. Why? Because Medicaid, unlike Medicare, pays for nursing home care for those who are poor enough (on paper at least), to qualify for the program. As this chapter will also detail, Medicaid provides other important health care benefits to its recipients.

Many people confuse Medicaid with Medicare. That's easy to understand. Both are governmentally-financed health care programs that are spelled and sound very much alike. However, in truth, the programs are very different.

The following are the major differences between Medicare and Medicaid:

| MEDICARE | MEDICAID |
|---|---|
| Medicare is designed primarily to assist senior citizens. | Medicaid assists people of all ages. |
| Medicare is not means-tested. It has the same benefits for the millionaire that it does for the senior living on Social Security. | Medicaid is available only to the poor. The exact definition of poor will vary, depending on the state in which you live. |
| Medicare is nationally financed. | The costs of Medicaid are paid jointly by the states and the federal government. |
| Medicare has uniform benefits and rules throughout the country. | Medicaid will have different eligibility rules and benefits in each state. |
| Medicare will not pay for custodial care in a nursing home. | Medicaid will pay for nursing home care. |
| Medicare is administered by the federal government. | Medicaid is administered by the states. |

## QUALIFYING FOR MEDICAID

The subject of qualifying for Medicaid cannot be as easily described as qualifying for Medicare. The rules of determining eligibility are often quite complicated and they differ in each state.

In general, you must meet certain income – and asset – level requirements to qualify for Medicaid. In some states, the level you must meet is based on your gross income. In other states, it's based on your net income.

If you exceed Medicaid eligibility requirements, you may be able to sell some of your assets to qualify. However, in states such as New Jersey, eligibility requirements are quite inflexible. For example, even after selling assets to try to qualify, a New Jersey resident with pension or Social Security benefits that exceed the income level is still precluded from Medicaid eligibility.

Even though Medicaid eligibility requirements vary from state-to-state, many of the key issues you need to be concerned about are similar throughout the nation. These include:

## Income Limits

You will not qualify for Medicaid if your income exceeds the maximum established by law in your state. This may seem like a simple matter. Either your earnings are small enough to qualify or they are not, right? Wrong. We are talking about the government here. Nothing in government bureaucracy is as it may seem. Moreover, the income that may qualify you for Medicaid benefits in New York may not in Mississippi.

If you qualify for *Supplemental Security Income* (see Chapter 9), you usually qualify for Medicaid. But not always. Some states have even more stringent eligibility requirements than is required to qualify for SSI. Then again, some are more liberal.

Many people think of income as money earned through employment or interest from investments. Under Medicaid, there is a much broader definition of the term. For example, a gift of money can be considered income. So can your Social Security check and money paid to you from a pension. In fact, any and all money that legally comes into your possession is countable as income under Medicaid unless specifically excluded by a state statute.

Your spouse's income may be counted too. For example, what happens if you have little income, but your spouse earns more than the maximum income allowed for Medicaid eligibility? If you are living with your spouse, you will not qualify for Medicaid because spousal income counts toward your eligibility, unless one of you permanently resides in a nursing home.

The person whose name is on the check is generally the person that is presumed to have received the income under most Medicaid programs. This issue is important when one spouse is in a nursing home. If your spouse's name is on the check and that spouse lives at home, his or her income will *not be counted* when determining Medicaid eligibility as long as you reside in a nursing home. This "name-on-the-check-rule" can save your spouse and your family a lot of money because it allows you to have nursing home care paid by Medicaid without forcing your at-home spouse to spend his or her income below the Medicaid eligibility level.

During the 1970's, some seniors lost their eligibility for Medicaid when they received their annual cost of living adjustment (COLA) in their Social Security benefits, bringing their incomes above the eligibility level for Medicaid. This was considered unfair because the Social Security COLAs were not a raise in income but were merely designed to keep Social Security recipients from losing ground due to inflation.

To prevent this injustice, Representative James Jarrell Pickle introduced an amendment to protect seniors from losing Medicaid benefits because of cost of living increases. Under the law, you are a "Pickle Person" and are allowed to remain on Medicaid if you would have been eligible for SSI but for the cost of living increases in your Social Security benefits. The effect of this law has been to greatly expand eligibility for Medicaid for people living on Social Security.

If you pay for private health insurance, your premium is deducted from your income before your eligibility is determined. If you have private health insurance, it pays before Medicaid steps in and Medicaid is only obliged to cover health care services not paid for by your policy. If you receive reimbursement directly from your health insurance, you will have to turn that money over to Medicaid if they paid benefits.

## Asset Limits

In addition to setting income limits, each state's Medicaid laws will establish a maximum value of assets that you can own and still be eligible for benefits. The maximum value varies from state-to-state, but typically falls within the $1,500 to $3,000 range. So, even if you have little or no income, you may remain ineligible for Medicaid if you own too much property. With regard to this important issue, you need to be aware of the following:

**The Assets Must Be Available.** For an asset to be counted against you, it must be "available." This means that you have the asset under your personal control or you can obtain it easily. If you cannot reach an asset or cash it in, the asset will be considered exempt. For example, if you own property in an economically-depressed area of the country and you can prove you've tried, but failed to sell it, it would probably not be counted in determining your eligibility for Medicaid.

**Your Homestead Is Exempt.** If you own and occupy your own home, you can still receive Medicaid. This remains true even if you enter a nursing home – as long as there is a reasonable expectation that you will be able to return to your home or have a spouse living at home. However, in most states, if it becomes clear that you will not be able to return home, your homestead will be treated as a countable asset which would probably cause you to lose your Medicaid eligibility. You would then have to sell your home and spend down the proceeds before you re-qualify for Medicaid assistance.

**Joint Bank Accounts Are Treated Differently in Each State.** Spouses often have joint bank accounts. Some states follow a rule that counts the entire account as an available asset when determining Medicaid eligibility. Others will only count one half of the account. If you think you or your spouse may need to go on Medicaid and you are worried that your joint account may affect your eligibility, you should find out your state's rules and take steps to separate your accounts if that should be necessary.

**Other Exempt Property.** The rules of Medicaid are not completely heartless. There are some types of property that you are allowed to keep without sacrificing your eligibility for benefits. These include:

- One automobile (there is usually no limit to the car's value)
- Furniture and household goods
- One wedding and engagement ring
- Life insurance with a face value of up to $1,500
- Burial plots

## RULES PROTECT YOUR SPOUSE'S SHARE OF THE PROPERTY

As with the rules regarding income, your spouse's assets may be treated as yours in determining eligibility. However, there are rules that prevent "spousal impoverishment" by protecting the well spouse's income and property (up to a certain asset level) who is not on Medicaid. The level of assets protected varies greatly from state-to-state. For more information, it's important to speak with someone knowledgeable about Medicaid.

## CATEGORICALLY NEEDY VS. MEDICALLY NEEDY

Many states have two standards of Medicaid eligibility. All states have a Medicaid program for those called the categorically needy. A person is categorically needy if they meet the income and asset eligibility requirements of their state.

Many states also allow people who are a little better off than those who are categorically needy to go on Medicaid. These people are known as the medically needy. Medically needy people are those who do not meet the minimum eligibility standards but who cannot pay for their own medical care. In such cases, medically needy people are permitted to spend the amount of income or assets they own above the Medicaid cut-off level on their own medical bills and go on the program. This is called spending down.

Otto lived in a state that only allowed categorically needy people to go on Medicaid. His income was $100 per month over the cut-off point for eligibility set by his state. Otto was unable to pay his medical bills and applied for Medicaid. He was rejected for coverage.

Otto's brother Oscar lived in an adjoining state that permitted medically needy seniors to go on Medicaid. Oscar also had an income that was $100 more than the cut-off point for eligibility. However, Oscar was permitted to spend the $100 on his own medical bills and go on Medicaid to help him pay the balance.

The distinction between being categorically needy and medically needy can be important for other reasons. Medically needy people may have to pay a small portion of the cost of their own health care and may receive fewer benefits. This will be discussed in more detail below.

## MEDICAID BENEFITS

Medicaid offers some important benefits to qualified beneficiaries, benefits that Medicare may not pay. Since the program is run at the state level, the total package of benefits will vary, depending on where you live.

Many people have questions about Medicaid benefits. The following are some of the most common:

### Do All Doctors Accept Medicaid Patients?

Unfortunately, no. In fact, you may have a difficult time finding a doctor who will accept Medicaid patients. Budget troubles have hit the Medicaid program like a hammer and some states have delayed payments to medical care providers, sometimes for months. Many doctors and other providers also complain they receive inadequate compensation for their services. In some areas, these and other problems have led to an acute shortage of medical professionals willing to take Medicaid recipients as patients. This is a problem that looks to get worse as federal and state governments cut budgets in the face of our growing national problem with public debt.

## What Health Care Is Paid by Medicaid?

There are different levels of benefits provided in different states. Since the federal government picks up a large part of the tab for Medicaid, it has mandated *minimum coverage* for the *categorically needy*. Some of these benefits exceed those offered by Medicare. These minimum benefits are as follows:

- Hospitalization
- Outpatient hospital services
- Physicians' services
- Lab tests and X-rays
- Nursing home care
- Home health care, including housekeeping care
- Transportation to and from the place you receive medical services

States are free to add additional benefits to their program if they choose to do so. Many states provide all or some of the following:

- Private-duty nursing
- Dental care
- Speech and occupational therapy
- Preventive health care services
- Eyeglasses and dentures
- Prescribed drugs
- Hospice services

## Do I Have to Pay for Any of My Health Care?

Not usually and if you do, it won't cost very much. Unlike Medicare, there is no distinction in Medicaid between accepting the assignment and not accepting the assignment. All Medicaid health care providers that participate in Medicaid receive their fees directly from Medicaid as payment in full. Moreover, they cannot bill you for covered services.

However, there are some areas where you may have to pay your state some additional charges. Here's a summary:

- If you are categorically needy, you cannot be charged for any of the federally mandated minimum services. However, if you receive a service that exceeds the minimum, your state can charge you a fee.
- States can and do charge fees for health services received by the medically needy on Medicaid. These fees can be a small sign-up charge when you enroll in the program, a copayment obligation or a small monthly premium. This is in addition to the spending down provision described above.

### Are Medicaid Benefits Ever Paid Retroactively?

Bureaucracies being what they are, a lot of time can pass between your application for Medicaid and your approval for benefits. This can place you in danger of having to pay for the high cost of medical care even though you have applied for Medicaid and are eligible for benefits. To prevent hardships caused by government red tape, the law allows your Medicaid coverage to extend up to three months back from the date your benefits begin. However, you must have met the eligibility requirements for those months.

## APPLYING FOR MEDICAID

You apply for Medicaid at your state's welfare department, health department or Social Security office. You can find out where to apply by making a telephone call to your local government welfare office, or by asking around at a senior center or other place where you find seniors and those who assist them. Look in the state government listings in your telephone book, under "health services." You can also call the: National Association of Area Agencies on Aging (NAAAA) at (800) 677-1116. This agency makes referrals to senior agencies and services across the country, such as: Social Security offices, Medicare and Medicaid offices, Meals on Wheels programs, legal assistance offices and more.

Applying for Medicaid is more complicated than applying for Medicare, since you have to provide details about your income and assets. Because the process can be very detailed, you will have a Medicaid eligibility worker assigned to help you sort through the rules.

You can make your worker's job (and yours) easier if you bring the following documents with you when you discuss your case the first time:

- Income Tax Returns for the last 30 months
- Paycheck stubs, if any
- Bank account records for the last 30 months
- Deeds to property you own
- Information about your spouse's finances
- Medical bills and records to confirm your medical situation
- The names, addresses and telephone numbers of doctors and/or hospitals that have provided you with care
- Your Social Security card or number
- Your driver's license, car registration and pink slip (the certificate of ownership) if you own a car
- Any other papers, such as statements from banks, brokers and pensions that will show how much income you have or how much property you own

Also, bring any information you believe will help you prove you should qualify for Medicaid as a "Pickle person" or someone who is medically needy, if you do not believe you will qualify as categorically needy.

Dealing with government bureaucrats and giving them so much detail about your life can be upsetting. Even though you will have an eligibility worker to help you, it is a good idea to bring a trusted friend or relative who knows the details of your finances and health, and who can assist you and your worker complete your application.

# MEDICAID COVERAGE AND NURSING HOMES

There is a very real and profound threat to the financial well being of seniors; the high cost of nursing home care. Some charge upwards of $2,500 per month or more for the full-time care they provide. Medicare does not pay for most nursing home care and it is the rare family that can withstand a prolonged drain of $2,500 per month or more without exhausting their assets. Many a life savings has been spent paying for nursing home care.

The good news is that careful planning may be able to preserve some or all of your property by legally getting Medicaid to pay for nursing home care. Since this book can only provide you with an overview of the subject of planning for Medicaid coverage for nursing home care, chances are you will want to consult a good lawyer to help you. *A word of warning:* Medicaid planning is not a place for amateurs. Lawyers who may be quite skilled in areas of the law such as divorce or bankruptcy or even estate planning may know little or nothing about Medicaid. Thus, if you decide to seek legal assistance, be sure to ask the lawyer if he or she is familiar with Medicaid law before you pay any money. Many lawyers familiar with Medicaid are members of the National Academy of Elder Law Attorneys. NAELA's administrative law office is located in Tucson, AZ. Their telephone number is: (602) 881-4005.

## Giving Away Property

At one time, an older person who believed he or she was going to have to need Medicaid would "give" his or her property to a trusted friend or family member. To prevent this, the government created rules penalizing gift *transfers* of non-exempt assets, such as stocks and bonds.

Such a transfer of non-exempt property will be considered invalid if it has taken place up to 30 months from the time you apply for Medicaid or, if you're already receiving Medicaid, during or after the 30-month period immediately prior to the date you entered the nursing home facility. The effect of such a transfer is to disqualify you for Medicaid qualification for a period of time. The ban from benefits can last for up to 30 months, depending on the specifics of your circumstances.

There are ways around the 30-month rule – if you plan ahead. If you believe that you or a loved one is likely to require nursing home care, now is the time to prepare for Medicaid eligibility. The sooner you plan, the more of your assets you may be able to retain.

There are several ways to legally arrange your affairs in order to plan for Medicaid. Here are four examples:

- You can sell property that Medicaid will count against eligibility, such as stocks and bonds, and use the money to invest in your exempt property such as a home or car. For example, you may own $50,000 worth of stock. You could sell it to pay off all or part of your mortgage.
- You can give away property to anyone, if you are certain not to need Medicaid nursing home support before the period of ineligibility expires.
- You can create a permanent trust, known as an *irrevocable living trust*, more than 30 months before going on Medicaid. (*Don't take this step lightly.* Once written, an irrevocable trust cannot be taken back.)
- You can purchase an annuity. In some states, certain types of annuities can be used as Medicaid planning devises. Make sure your state allows annuities to be used in this way.

One other point: If you give away property, sell it or otherwise engage in transactions to plan for Medicaid eligibility, beware of the tax man. Property transfers or liquidations may create a *taxable event* under the law. For example, if you sell stock, you may have to pay a capital gains tax. If you give away more than $10,000 in property, there may be a gift tax owed. The tax codes are very complicated and designed to raise money for the government whenever possible. Be sure and check with your lawyer or accountant before transferring property to see if there is a tax consequence to the transfer.

Here's how this works with regard to the most commonly-owned asset:

**Your Home.** From our earlier discussion, you will recall that your homestead is usually exempt from being counted as an asset when determining eligibility for Medicaid. However, if you live alone in your home and enter a nursing home without the likelihood that you will ever be able to live in your home again, the asset loses its exemption.

To avoid this unhappy result, you can keep your home in the family by transferring title under the following limited circumstances:

- To your spouse who is still living at home. This can be important in preserving the home for your children, since your spouse may, in some states, transfer the house to your children.
- To a minor child (through a *guardianship* or trust) or to a blind or disabled child.
- To a child of any age who has lived with you and cared for you for two years prior to your admission into a nursing home, if the care delayed your admission to the nursing home.
- To a sibling who already has an ownership interest in the property and who has lived in the home for at least the previous year.

Otto was diagnosed with a long-term debilitating disease. Because of the diagnosis, he knew that he would probably have to enter a nursing home for custodial care. He asked his daughter, Sarah, if she would live with him and care for him. In return, he would transfer title of his house to her. She cared for her father for two years before he was forced to enter the nursing home. Her care had prevented an earlier admission. Otto applied for Medicaid. Despite the fact that he would never return home, and the fact that the transfer occurred fewer than 30 months before his admission, putting Sarah's name on the title to the home was not considered a gift transfer and he was allowed into the Medicaid program.

Oscar was diagnosed with the same disease and had to enter a nursing home and had little likelihood that he would again be able to live in his house. Oscar was married to Edna. When he went into the nursing home, she continued to live in the house. Because she continued to live in the house, the property was considered exempt and Oscar qualified for Medicaid.

Oscar and Otto's long-time friend Oren was also diagnosed with a debilitating disease and had to leave his home of 50 years. Oren never married or had children. Before entering a nursing home he transferred his house to a distant cousin because he knew he would not be returning home. The transfer was not considered valid by Medicaid because it took place fewer than 30 months from the time he applied to Medicaid as a nursing home resident and because valid transfers can only take place between home owners and their children or siblings. Oren was refused Medicaid benefits.

# IF YOU ARE DENIED MEDICAID

If you are denied Medicaid and you believe the turn-down was in error, you can appeal the decision. The rules of appeal vary from state-to-state but in every state you will be allowed to present testimony, supply evidence, have witnesses appear on your behalf and, if you want, have a representative to help you at the hearing. *Your representative does not have to be a lawyer.* Also note, there may be a short time limit for your appeal. So don't wait. If you delay, you may lose your right to appeal.

For more details on Medicaid appeals, contact your state welfare or social services office, or speak with a lawyer who practices in the field of elder law. Also, contact your local multi-purpose senior center or call NAAAA's hotline listed on page 59.

# 6

# VETERANS' BENEFITS

The generation that spent its formative years during the depression and the war years of the 1940's is now in its senior years. Most men and many women of that era are veterans, having served during World War II and during the Korean Conflict. For many veterans, your service gives you legal rights to health care provided through the Department of Veterans Affairs (DVA). This may be true even if you did not receive an Honorable Discharge. This can be important because of the benefit and coverage gaps that exist in Medicare, especially if you are over the age of 65, have too high an income to qualify for Medicaid and cannot otherwise afford to pay for your health care.

The promise of veterans' health care that shined so brightly after World War II has dimmed. The number of veterans who receive real benefit from these programs is limited. In the real world, budget constraints keep all but the very poor or those veterans with service-related maladies from receiving care. Lack of accessibility is also a problem for veterans living in a locale without a large veterans' hospital. Finally, some dislike the long lines and crowded conditions that exist in many veterans' health care facilities. Still, if you are a veteran, age 65 or older and otherwise unable to pay for your health care, you may be entitled to priority care with the Department of Veterans Affairs.

## QUALIFYING FOR VETERANS' BENEFITS

If you are a veteran or the family member of a veteran, you probably qualify for benefits. That's the good news. The bad news, as discussed below, is that mere qualification may not be enough to get you access to treatment.

On the issue of qualification, as opposed to the issue of actually receiving benefits, the following general standards apply:

- You must have been in the Armed Forces of the United States of America. Allied service does not count, nor does civilian defense-related service.
- You cannot have received a dishonorable discharge. Many people believe that a veteran must have been honorably discharged in order to qualify for benefits. While that is true of some DVA programs, it is only the Dishonorable Discharge that disqualifies you for health benefits.
- You may have to have suffered a service-connected disability or injury: Injury in service to country is a threshold qualification for many health care benefits, such as hospitalization or nursing home care. This is the same for obtaining benefits for your family members.

## VETERAN HEALTH CARE BENEFITS

The health care benefits available through the Department of Veterans Affairs come as close to pure socialized medicine as we get in this country. The medical facilities are owned by the government and the doctors are paid by the government. Patients pay little or nothing for their own care. This is particularly true of the Department of Veterans Affairs hospitals and clinics that offer a wide array of free or very low-cost health care services for qualified veterans and their dependents.

There are more than 150 veterans' hospitals and clinics throughout the United States, with a bed capacity exceeding 100,000. At the same time, there are millions of qualified people to be served. Because the available supply of health care does not come near to meeting the potential demand for services, the DVA has instituted a *priority system,* which is used to determine who will receive care first.

You receive priority care if you are an otherwise qualified veteran and if:

- You are rated service-connected: In other words, your illness or injury was suffered in connection with your military service.
- You are retired from active duty because of a disability you incurred or aggravated while in the military.
- You are receiving a DVA pension.
- You are a former POW.
- You are an "atomic veteran," i.e., you participated in the atomic bomb tests.
- You are eligible for Medicaid.
- You are considered a "low income" veteran and thus unable to pay for care. (In 1993, the maximum income permitted for in-patient care was $19,408 if you were single and $23,290 if you had one dependent. That isn't very much, but it is significantly more than you can earn and receive to qualify for Medicaid.)

It is also important to note that there are priorities within the priorities. First priority goes to emergencies and to people already receiving treatment. Thereafter, veterans with service-connected conditions go to the front of the line. Then come patients who are receiving, or who are eligible to receive, DVA disability compensation and who need treatment for a nonservice-related condition. Last on the priority list, but still ahead of the rest of the pack, are veterans and their dependents who are age 65 and unable to pay for treatment anywhere else.

If you are not eligible for priority care and have a low income, you may still be admitted to a hospital on a space-available status. If you are a veteran who is not low-income and is non-priority, you can be admitted if there is space, but you will have to pay for your care. However, you cannot be forced to pay more than the Part A Medicare deductible, which was $676 in 1993 plus half of that deductible ($338) times three in any given year, approximately $1,690.

---

Otto, a veteran of World War II, had been called back into service during the Korean Conflict. He had been assigned to the atomic testing grounds in Nevada, where he lost his hearing during an atom bomb blast. As a result, he was given a service-related disability discharge. Years later, he developed lung cancer. He was given priority status because of his service-connected disability and because he was an atomic veteran, and was immediately admitted to the local Veterans' Hospital for surgery and other treatment, which he received free of charge.

Otto's brother Oscar, had served in World War II and in Korea. He suffered from malaria in World War II but recovered fully. He was wounded in Korea but luckily, his injury had not been serious and he had served out the balance of his time in the military without further incident. Oscar also came down with lung cancer but was not a priority case, despite his Purple Heart. He was put on a waiting list and told he would have to pay for part of his care. Since his doctor strongly advised against waiting, Oscar decided to get his care paid by Medicare.

---

The DVA also offers long-term care for veterans needing skilled nursing care. You can qualify for this care if you must be treated for *any* disability, so long as you have a service-related disability. For example, if you lost your arm in an explosion during the war, you have a service-related disability. If you subsequently suffer a stroke and require skilled nursing, you will qualify, even though the condition being treated is not service-related.

Usually, the skilled nursing facility care must be provided at a VA facility, but this is not always the case. For example, if you have a service-related disability or impairment requiring medical care and you are low income and there is no DVA facility available to meet your needs, the DVA may pay a private nursing facility to provide your care.

If you are admitted into a DVA nursing home and you receive a DVA disability pension, the DVA may reduce your pension benefits while you live in the home if you do not have a dependent living in the community. Also, custodial care is usually not available through the DVA.

Some veterans need assistance that is less intensive than hospitalization or nursing home care but more so than in-home health care. For these veterans, the DVA has a limited number of domiciliaries available to assist them. Domiciliaries offer shelter, food, clothing and other comforts of home, along with medical care. Domiciliaries can make the difference between home and homelessness, since qualification for admission is strictly limited to veterans who have little or no income.

The DVA has also joined the home health care movement, offering home health care to qualified veterans who are recovering from surgery, an acute illness or injury.

In order to receive home health care, you must be served by a home health care unit that works for the DVA. Unlike skilled nursing home care, the DVA will not pay an outside agency for home health care if you need it. However, there is an exception to this general rule: If you have a severe service-related disability, you *may* be able to obtain outside help – but only if the DVA gives its approval in advance.

The DVA may offer other benefits in your area. Adult day care services exist in some localities; dental services and rehabilitation programs and hospice facilities exist in some hospitals.

## APPEALING DENIAL OF CLAIMS

If you've been denied coverage, you can appeal to the Board of Veterans Appeals (BVA). But first you must submit a letter indicating a notice of disagreement to the facility that denied your benefit. The facility will reconsider your claim. If they deny it again, they're required to send you a complete report on your case and information and forms on how to appeal their decision to the BVA.

At the BVA, you can elect to have a third person of your choice assist you. Many private veterans' organizations, such as the Disabled American Veterans, assist veterans and their kin prepare their cases for the Board.

If you lose at the Board level, you can file an appeal with the United States Court of Veterans Appeal. The appeal must be filed within 120 days of the date of the notice of the Board decision. If you can afford to hire a lawyer to assist you at this level, he or she will be permitted to charge you a reasonable fee for the representation. The amount of the fee will depend on the work performed and the complexity of the case. Your attorney's fee must be approved by the court. (At one time lawyers were limited to charging $10 for services to veterans in DVA matters. The law was passed after the Civil War when $10 was a lot more money than it is today. Lawyers can still only charge $10 for representing you at the BVA level, although third parties, such as a relative or friend, can pay your lawyer more.)

For further information, contact your local office of the Department of Veterans Affairs. It can be found by looking in your telephone book under U.S. Government, or you can contact a veterans' support organization in your area.

# 7

# ISSUES OF LIFE & DEATH

The actor Guy Stockwell tells the true story of a "white knuckle" plane ride he once took. He was sitting next to a businessman who became quite upset as turbulence caused the plane to buck and pitch. Finally the scared man exclaimed, "If I die, it's not going to be in a plane crash!" Guy looked at him, chuckled and said, "What do you mean, 'If'. . .?" The man gave Guy a horrified look and refused to speak to him the rest of the flight.

Death is a fact of life that most of us try to ignore as we go about our daily lives. But there comes a time when, ready or not, we must face the reality of our own mortality. This is of immediate concern to older people who, by definition, have reached life's later stages.

For many seniors, death is not the primary worry. Rather, many will tell you that their greatest fear is not dying but losing control of their own bodies by being kept uselessly alive against their will by the miracle machines of modern medicine.

This is not a matter of paranoia. Most people have heard stories of a hopelessly ill old person who has been brought back from death through resuscitation or other "extraordinary" means, only to die soon again. Some estimate that as many as 10,000 people are being kept alive in a "persistent vegetative" state in the United States. For many, this prospect sounds worse than torture.

The medical and legal communities have come to recognize the ethical dilemma presented by the right of people to control their own health and the medical profession's obligation to keep people alive. The result: Increasingly, you have the power to decide ahead of time the nature and extent of the medical care you will receive when your time comes.

This chapter discusses the legal tools you can use to control the decisions surrounding your death, including: your right to refuse care, *living wills*, and the *durable power of attorney for health care.*

## INFORMED CONSENT AND INFORMED REFUSAL

To a large degree, you have always had a great deal of legal control over these medical decisions. Despite how it often feels, your doctor is not the king or queen and you are not the vassal subject to the royal whim. You have always had the decision-making power over your own health care, not your doctor. You are legally entitled to what is known as *informed consent* and *informed refusal.*

Decisions that must be made about your own medical care start and end with you, as long as you are mentally competent to make the decision. Your doctor's job is not to order you around but to tell you the truth about your medical condition, explain the treatment options available, and describe the pros and cons of tests and proposed treatments. You then have the right to decide what to do. This is known under the law as informed consent. Legally, you cannot be treated without your permission, or if you are incapacitated, without the consent of a close relative, an emergency court order or another person legally entitled to make the decision.

Just as you have to consent to treatment before it can be provided, you also have the right to refuse treatment altogether. If you are seriously ill or injured and your doctor recommends a course of treatment, you don't have to go along. Instead, you can refuse treatment, get another doctor or decide on some other course, and go from there.

> Otto was diagnosed with advanced lung cancer. He was told that the best treatment available was the removal of a lung, extensive chemotherapy and radiation treatment, which would make him quite ill and which ultimately had little chance to save his life. Otto decided to give his informed consent to the medical treatment required to fight for his life.
>
> Otto's brother Oscar received the same diagnosis. He decided that the quality of his life would be better without invasive surgery and toxic treatment, and that he preferred to live out the balance of his life in as much comfort and dignity as possible. He gave his informed refusal to the treatment, deciding instead, to receive hospice treatment to keep him as comfortable and pain free as possible. His wishes were honored by his family and his doctors.

The laws of informed consent and informed refusal give you a great deal of power over your own quality of life and the circumstances of your own death. If your doctor wants you to undergo treatment that will cause you great discomfort or pain, you can say no or you can agree. You are in control. It is the law. (If your doctor disagrees with your decision, he or she can ask you to find another doctor, but medical care cannot be withdrawn until you have found a new physician.)

The real problem for many people comes when because of illness or injury, you are physically or mentally incapable of deciding for yourself. For example, if you suffer a stroke and are in a coma, what then? Must you be attached to a machine and kept alive even if there is little or no hope? Must doctors and your family subject you to the indignity of being forced to breathe by a machine and fed through a plastic tube? Or is there a way for you to exercise informed consent or informed refusal even when you cannot legally decide for yourself?

In recent years, legal tools have become increasingly utilized to allow you to plan ahead so that you can still have your say about your own treatment, even if incapacitated.

## LIVING WILLS

Living wills are short, simple documents instructing your doctors and your family as to the extent of treatment you wish to receive if you are near death and unable to give your own informed consent or refusal.

A new federal law, the "Patient Self-Determination Act" requires hospitals, HMOs, nursing homes and other health-care providers to bring up the subject of living wills to prospective patients. The purpose of the law is to educate the public about the use of these documents, although a patient cannot be refused medical treatment or admission to a nursing home simply because they don't have or want a living will.

In essence, a living will allows you to decide ahead of time whether or not you want to be resuscitated should your heart stop beating, have a respirator assist your breathing if you cannot breathe for yourself, or have other medical treatment rendered to save your life when you are *hopelessly* ill or injured. Typically, a living will is used to request that life-sustaining equipment be disconnected when there is virtually no chance of your recovery. As you might expect in an issue involving life, death and the law, people often have questions. Here are the most common:

### Are Living Wills Legally Binding?

The laws of the "right to die" are different in each state. Some states permit you to legally refuse all life-prolonging treatment through your living will and compel your doctors to honor your directive. Three states – Massachusetts, Michigan and New York – have no living will legislation. However, written living wills or statements can still provide legal evidence of your wishes. To find out the law in your state, contact your Area Agency on Aging, your local chapter of the AARP, the New York based non-profit group, Choice in Dying, or ask your attorney.

## What Is the Meaning of "Terminal Condition?"

Living wills come into play when your condition is considered terminal and you cannot make medical decisions for yourself. At first glance, a terminal condition means a condition where death is predictably imminent. But what about comas and persistent vegetative states? People can live for years in such a condition. Some states allow an irreversible coma and a persistent vegetative state to be considered terminal conditions for purposes of carrying out instructions in a living will. Regardless of its binding nature, if you are unsure of the law in your state, you may want to specifically address this issue in your living will. This, at least, will inform your relatives what you want.

## Any Medical Procedures Excluded?

Some states require specific mention of your wishes regarding the use of artificial feeding and hydration. You would be wise to specifically mention your wishes about these particular treatments. Again, even if not binding in your state, it alerts your loved ones about your wishes.

## How Do I Prepare a Living Will?

Happily, living wills are easy to prepare, but great care should be given when writing your instructions. This is especially important when you consider that decisions based on your living will literally involve your life or death. Several books have information on living wills complete with sample forms. You may also wish to discuss the matter with your attorney. If you decide to prepare your own living will, there are state-specific fill-in-the-blank forms, complete with instructions, available from Choice in Dying. Pay careful attention to the details when filling one out.

Whether you hire an attorney or prepare the living will yourself, keep in mind that you should include:

- Your wishes concerning the use of artificial feeding and hydration.
- Your definition of a terminal condition.
- How you want to be treated – or not treated – if you are in a coma or a persistent vegetative state (i.e. do you want a respirator?, etc.).
- If you want pain to be controlled, even if it means you would be semi-conscious or unaware of your surroundings or if it would hasten your death.
- How long you wish your life to be sustained by artificial means such as a respirator, if you decide you want medical technology to keep you alive.
- Whether you want resuscitation should you experience heart or respiratory failure.

### Can I Change My Living Will?

Yes, anytime you want to by destroying the old living will and writing a new one.

## DURABLE POWER OF ATTORNEY

A living will permits you to state ahead of time how you want to be treated should you become terminally ill. A Durable Power of Attorney for Health Care is somewhat different. It permits you to grant someone the power to make important heath care decisions on your behalf should you be unable to make them yourself. These documents also allow you to tell the person you name, known as your *attorney-in-fact* or *health-care proxy*, what your desires are regarding extraordinary care.

The majority of states and Washington, D.C., now permit health care powers of attorney. Although stationery stores carry forms for appointing a durable power of attorney for financial purposes, some states require a specific form for appointing a health-care agent. Many lawyers will draft either of these documents at a very low cost, as a courtesy for long-term clients or as part of their services in preparing an overall estate plan.

If you prepare a Durable Power of Attorney for Health Care, remember the following:

- The document must meet the particularities of your state's laws, including form and content.
- The document will require witnessing but witnessing requirements vary from state-to-state. It may also require notarization.
- You can rescind the power of attorney at any time by destroying the document or preparing a new one.

## OTHER FORMS OF DECISION MAKING

Here are two examples of other ways to control your medical destiny:

### "Do Not Resuscitate" Orders

Heart attacks and respiratory failure treated by heart resuscitation may include the administration of electric shocks to the heart. That is well and good. But what if you are terminally ill without hope of recovery and the resuscitation merely prolongs your agony? If you are terminally ill, New York and Florida allow you to legally direct that no resuscitation be attempted. In many states, this is often handled in an informal manner.

### Surrogate Decision Making

If you do not prepare a living will or Durable Power of Attorney for Health Care, a guardianship may have to be established, or the family may have to go to court seeking a judge's order allowing life-sustaining treatment to be withheld. This can be emotionally and financially draining.

Some states have recently created "surrogate decision-making statutes," which set in law the order of priority for the person or entity allowed to make medical decisions. The hierarchy usually begins with you, moves to a judicially-appointed guardian, to a person named in a power of attorney and then, to relatives. Some states have established medical boards to make these decisions in the absence of legal-consent authority having been placed in anyone else.

---

Otto was told by his doctors that he was terminally ill with cancer and that, in all probability, he had but a few months to live. He immediately signed a living will in a state where the law recognized the legality of the document. In his living will, Otto directed that no extraordinary measures be taken to save his life. When his time came, the doctors abided by his wishes and did not put him through resuscitation or put him on a respirator, and he died peacefully in his sleep.

Otto's brother Oscar, was diagnosed with the same condition and had the same prognosis. He did not live in a state that recognized living will. However, his state had authorized durable powers of attorney for health care. He prepared a living will directing that he was not to be resuscitated or put on a respirator to save his life. He also prepared a Durable Power of Attorney for Health Care, with the same instructions, naming his daughter as surrogate decision-maker. When his time came, his daughter was legally permitted to direct his doctors not to take extraordinary measures to save his life.

---

## EUTHANASIA AND ASSISTED SUICIDE

There is a difference between withholding treatment and actively assisting another to take their own lives or to kill them with their consent. In this chapter, we have discussed the withholding of life-sustaining care (sometimes called passive euthanasia). Killing someone or assisting them to commit suicide is "euthanasia" (sometimes referred to as active euthanasia). The difference: In the former, nature is "allowed to take its course." In the latter, someone intervenes to hasten the death process, such as through a lethal injection.

A growing political and social movement in the country seeks to legalize physician-assisted suicide and active euthanasia for the terminally ill. As of this writing, all forms of "active" euthanasia remains a criminal homicide in every state. Killing someone at their request, sometimes called mercy killing, is usually treated as murder by state courts.

One can expect euthanasia to be in the headlines for years to come, as Americans seek to come to grips with the morality and emotions surrounding this issue.

# PART 2

# INCOME BENEFITS

# 8

# SOCIAL SECURITY–
# AN OVERVIEW

In these days of ubiquitous government agencies and talk of the "welfare state," it may be hard to believe that the granddaddy of all social welfare programs, Social Security, is less than sixty years old. In fact, someone born on the day the program became the law of the land, would not yet qualify for Social Security retirement benefits.

Social Security is really three income programs in one. Although most people think of Social Security as a retirement program, it is also a disability insurance program, as well as an annuity program for dependents and survivors of beneficiaries. You or your family may qualify for any or all of these differing programs at different times in your lives. This chapter introduces you to Social Security and deals with issues of qualifying for the program. The next chapter will detail the different benefits available to you under Social Security and the income booster for many poor people, Supplemental Security Income (SSI).

Social Security is administered by the Social Security Administration (SSA), which is part of the U.S. Department of Health and Human Services. Like Medicare, it was created by federal law, and the rules are the same throughout the country.

Social Security is not financed through the general fund made up of income and other federal taxes. Rather, a specific payroll tax (FICA) is collected, one half from workers and one half from employers. Those who are self-employed have to pay both the employer's and employee's portion of the FICA tax based on their net earnings.

Currently, more money is collected through FICA taxes than is paid out in benefits. This is done by design. The surplus funds are supposed to build-up the Social Security Trust Fund, pending the large increase in recipients that can be expected when the Baby Boom generation reaches retirement age. However, the money held in trust is being borrowed by the government to help mask the true magnitude of the budget deficit and the extent of the national debt. Some critics fear that this will ultimately bankrupt the Social Security system.

When you start to collect benefits, you will receive your Social Security check on or about the third of each month. Checks are sent by U.S. Mail. However, the best and safest way to receive your money is to have it paid directly into your bank account. If you don't have a bank account, it may be worth opening one just to receive the assurance that come rain, sleet, snow or human error, you will receive your money on time. Ask your bank for details.

## FACTS ABOUT SOCIAL SECURITY

Before looking at the specifics of applying for Social Security, there are some important things you should know about the program:

### You Do Not Have to Be 65 to Collect Benefits

Some people confuse the rules of Medicare with the rules of Social Security, and thus believe you have to be 65 to qualify for Social Security. This is not true. While the majority of recipients are senior citizens, people of many ages can receive Social Security benefits. For example, survivor's benefits can be paid to children, disability pay-

ments are often paid to younger workers and even retirement benefits can be paid beginning at age 62.

Social Security was designed as an income *supplement*,
and not a substitute for pensions, interest earnings or life
savings. That is why it is so difficult for those seniors whose
sole means of support is their Social Security, to make ends
meet.

## Most Workers Are Covered by Social Security Law

The scope of Social Security coverage has expanded over
the years. Many workers, such as those working for
government entities, at one time did not pay into the Social
Security system. That has changed. Today fully 95 percent
of people in the work force must pay FICA taxes and are, in
turn, covered by the program.

## Social Security Benefits May Be Taxed

If you earn enough money through other sources
(approximately $25,000 if single; $32,000 if filing jointly in
1993), your Social Security retirement benefits may be
subject to an income tax. Once you begin to receive benefits,
you will receive a statement from Social Security each
January recapping your previous year's benefit payments
and a form explaining how to report your Social Security
income to the IRS.

## Benefits Can Be Lost If You Have Outside Earnings

If you are receiving Social Security benefits and you
earn money through work, you have to report the earnings
to the SSA. If you are under age 65, and your earnings
exceed the limit set by SSA ($7,680 in 1993), you will begin
to lose benefits at the rate of one dollar for every two dollars
earned. If you are between 65 and 69 and your earnings
exceed $10,560, you lose benefits at the rate of one dollar for
every three dollars earned. However, if you are 70 or over,
you can work and collect all of your benefits.

## You Need to Reimburse Overpayment of Benefits

If you receive more money from Social Security than you are entitled to under the law, the SSA can demand to be reimbursed and can deduct money from your future benefit checks to enforce their claim. However, if you can show that the overpayment was *not your fault* and it would be unfair, given your finances, to force you to repay the money, you may be able to keep the extra money you received.

## You Will Receive a COLA Each Year

Each year your benefits will be raised a percentage based on the rate of inflation. Thus, if the cost of living goes up two percent, so will your benefits. However, COLAs (Cost of Living Adjustment) are a likely target of budget cutters, at least for the better-off Social Security recipients, as the government strives to reduce the budget deficit and lower the national debt.

## You Can Claim Benefits Under a Divorced Spouse's Work Record

If you were married for more than 10 years and never remarried, you can claim benefits under your former spouse's work record. Before doing so, however, check whether you will receive a higher benefit by applying under your own name.

## Benefits May Not Be Garnished by Creditors

This rule applies even if the creditor is a governmental entity, except, of course, for the payment of back taxes. Social Security can also be attached to enforce child support orders or alimony.

## You May Name Someone to Receive Your Money

Usually Social Security is paid directly to the *beneficiary*. However, if you are incompetent and unable to handle your own affairs, a designated payee can be named to receive your money on your behalf.

# HOW YOUR BENEFITS ARE COMPUTED

Before getting into exactly what benefits you may be entitled to, this section introduces you to the basics of computing benefits. Whether you qualify for the program and if so, the amount of money you will receive from Social Security, is dependent on the money you earned and the time you spent on-the-job over your working life.

In order to qualify for Social Security you must have worked a long enough time and had minimum earnings, measured as *quarters of coverage*. The number of quarters you need to qualify for Social Security depends on which Social Security program is being applied for. Veterans may qualify for extra quarters for their service in the military.

Once you have earned sufficient quarters to qualify for Social Security, the amount of money you receive depends on the amount of money you or your spouse earned during your working years. This amount is called the Primary Insurance Amount (PIA). Figuring out your own PIA is a mathematical formula which factors in your age at the time you start receiving your benefits, your Average Indexed Monthly Income (AIMI) and the time you apply.

Currently, a worker needs a total of 40 quarters to receive retirement benefits and can earn a maximum of four quarters in each year. In 1993, one quarter equaled $590. If a W-2 form showed an annual earning of more than $2,360 ($590 times four quarters), the worker still only earned four quarters that year toward the actual 40 needed to collect his or her retirement benefits.

If you are under age 60 and want to figure out how many quarters you've earned toward retirement benefits, ask your local Social Security office to send you a Form 7004 Personal Earnings and Benefit Statement. (If you're over 60, you don't have to write. You can call you local Social Security office for a benefits estimate.) In return, you will receive a free computerized printout which will supply the following information:

- A year-to-year breakdown of your earnings.
- The amount of Social Security taxes you have paid.
- The current-dollar estimate of the retirement benefits you will receive. (The estimate will give you figures for retirement at age 62, 65 and 67, each of which will bring you a different figure. See Chapter 9.)

It is important to get your PIA as you plan for retirement, since this information will help you plan your retirement date and post-retirement family budget. Moreover, the Social Security Administration (SSA) has been known to make mistakes. (It was once reported that the SSA had nearly $60 billion dollars less in total earnings credited to FICA taxpayers than did the IRS.)

It is important to use the Benefits Statement to correct any errors in your account, since under-crediting of income will reduce your benefits. You only have a *three-year window* of opportunity to make corrections, so it is a good idea to make periodic checks of your records to make sure they are accurate.

## APPLYING FOR SOCIAL SECURITY

Many people, especially those who are older, get intimidated when dealing with government agencies. This need not happen to you. While the office may seem very busy, just remember, your tax dollars have gone to make sure the people at Social Security are there to help. The following are common questions asked by people who are about to apply for Social Security:

## Where Do I Go to Apply?

You should apply for Social Security in person at your local Social Security office. The address and telephone number will be in the blue pages of your telephone book under United States Government listings.

## When Should I Apply?

If you are applying for retirement benefits, you should apply two to three months prior to when you want the benefits to begin. This is especially true if applying before you are age 65, since you will not receive back payments for benefits missed because you were late applying. However, after age 65, you can receive up to six months back benefits. If you are applying for disability or survivor's benefits, apply as soon as you believe you are eligible.

## What Should I Bring With Me?

Paperwork is the name of the game when applying for Social Security. You will have to prove, through documentation, that the information you supply is true. Thus, you should be sure to bring the following documents with you (keeping copies safely at home in case your file somehow gets lost in the shuffle) when you go in to apply.

- Your Social Security card or number.
- If you are applying as a dependent or survivor (see Chapter 9), the Social Security card or number of the person under whose name and work record you are applying.
- Your proof of age, such as a birth certificate, baptismal certificate or any other document that will prove your age.
- If you are a widowed person applying as a dependent or survivor, your marriage certificate to the person under whose name and work record you are applying and a death certificate.

- Your last few years of W-2 forms or federal income tax returns.
- Proof of military service, if any.
- If applying for disability benefits, proof of your claim, such as doctor's records.

If you've lost these records, try to get copies. For example, if you know where you were born, the local Hall of Records or Clerk of Court should have a copy of your birth certificate. If you can't obtain copies, discuss the matter with your Social Security case worker.

Be prepared to assist your case worker in any way possible. And make sure that any other communications made about your application are made in writing, and be sure you keep copies of all such communications. In that way, if something goes wrong, you will have proof that you applied and that you supplied all of the information asked of you.

## APPEALING A DENIAL OF CLAIMS

If you apply for Social Security and are rejected or find that your benefits are lower than the amount to which you believe you are entitled, you can – and should – appeal. It is the rare appeal that succeeds but then again, yours may be the one that succeeds.

The first formal step in the appeal process is to file a written document requesting that the original Social Security decision, called a determination, be reconsidered. This process is called the "Request for Reconsideration." You have 60 days from the date you receive the original written decision, so be sure not to "sit on your rights" and end up losing them. Your local Social Security office will have the forms you need.

A Reconsideration is not a formal process. Rather, it is simply a second look at your case by a different case worker than the person who made the original decision in your case. The whole process is done at the Social Security office based only on the documents in your file, so if you have any new evidence you wish to have placed in your file, this is the time to get it into your file. Once you have filed your request, there is nothing further for you to do but wait and see if the outcome is more to your liking.

If you remain dissatisfied with the result of your Reconsideration and you still want to appeal, the next step is to demand a formal administrative hearing. Again, don't sit on your rights. You only have 60 days from receiving written notice of the results of the Reconsideration to file for the hearing.

Before attending your hearing, exercise your right to compare your file at the Social Security office with the documents you possess and make sure that nothing is missing from your official file that would adversely affect the outcome of the appeal.

The hearing will be scheduled for a specific day and time. While you can ask to have it rescheduled, it is a good idea to put the hearing at the top of your priority list so that your result will not be delayed. The hearing, unlike the Reconsideration, will be held in front of an administrative law judge. The atmosphere will not be as formal as a court room but it will not be an informal chat either. You can present testimony and can have a lawyer or lay advocate at the hearing to assist you in your presentation.

The next step up the ladder of appeals is a request for a hearing by the National Social Security Appeals Council in Washington, D.C. Few people go this far in appealing Social Security decisions and fewer still, succeed. Still, if you want to sue the government, you will have to take this step. You have 60 days from receiving the written decision of the hearing to file your request. Chances are there will not be a formal hearing held at this level, and if there is, it will be in Washington, D.C., and you may not be able to afford to attend.

If you literally want to make a federal case out of your situation, once you have exhausted your Social Security in-house administrative remedies, you are entitled to file a formal lawsuit in Federal District Court. This lawsuit will be a very formal event. Not only will you have to know the law, but you will have to understand court procedure. That is, you will have to know and abide by "the way things are done" in the court. Procedure can be difficult to master –

even for lawyers – so unless you are prepared to take a great deal of time and effort learning procedure as well as the law, it is a good idea to hire a lawyer to represent you. At the very least, you should consult a lawyer to see if your view of the law is correct and that you have a viable opportunity to win your case.*

## GETTING HELP

Standing up to the government can be a daunting task. But fear not. Help is available from many sources:

### Senior Advocates

Many multipurpose senior centers and senior citizen organizations have volunteer Social Security experts to help you prepare your Social Security appeals and even assist you at administrative hearings. The service is usually free and thus it is a good idea to seek assistance even if you think you know what you are doing.

### Friends or Family

Moral support and hand-holding can be very important in times of stress. Happily, during the SSA administrative appeals, you can have anyone you want assist you, including a son, a daughter or a friend. They can also speak on your behalf with the people at Social Security or at an administrative hearing. If you have such a trusted friend or relative, now may be the time to ask for help.

---

* For tips on hiring and working with lawyers, see *Using a Lawyer*, by Kay Ostberg, in association with HALT, Random House, 1990, $8.95.

## Free Clinics

Some law schools and community clinics have volunteer lawyers or law students who can help you with your Social Security questions. Most charge little or no fee for their services.

## Lawyers

Last but not least, some attorneys specialize in work related to Social Security and Medicare. If there is a lot of money at stake in your case, seriously consider consulting a lawyer. Fortunately, if you retain a lawyer to assist you, you will be protected by the court from being charged an unreasonable fee.

# ATTORNEYS FEES AND SOCIAL SECURITY

If you decide to retain an attorney to represent you, make sure that he or she is knowledgeable in the law of Social Security and in the procedures of going about seeking justice on your behalf. Relatively few lawyers practice in this field, so make sure you take the time to find the right lawyer.

When it comes to fees, unlike most attorney-client situations, the attorney cannot charge you whatever he or she may believe the market will bear. Instead, the fee must be approved as "reasonable" by the Social Security Administration or the court. (Some attorneys will ask for an up-front fee, called a retainer. If yours does, the law compels the lawyer to keep the fee in an escrow account, pending the approval of the fee that will be charged.)

The actual amount of the fee will depend on the complexity of the case, the extent of services performed, the skill and competence of your lawyer and the results achieved for you. If the case involved collecting past due benefits, the fee will generally be 25 percent of the amount collected on your behalf.

At the end of the case, your attorney submits a fee request to the Social Security Administration or the court, depending on whether there has been a case in court. He or she must serve you with a copy of this document. If you believe the request is wrong or unreasonable, speak up. You have the absolute right to have your voice heard. After all, it is your money that is at stake.

# 9

# SOCIAL SECURITY BENEFITS & SSI

This chapter discusses the benefits side of the Social Security equation. Social Security provides a vital income supplement for millions of Americans of all ages and for some, constitutes their sole means of support. Social Security represents one of the biggest items in the United States budget, constituting 27 percent of all money spent by the federal government.

## RETIREMENT BENEFITS

The most famous Social Security program and the one most senior citizens use, is the retirement benefit. You qualify for the retirement benefit if you are age 62 or older, and have earned sufficient quarters. If you earned enough quarters to qualify for retirement benefits, the amount of your monthly benefit will be based on the age at which you apply and the average income you earned during all of your working years.

The age you choose to apply for benefits will have a major impact on the amount of money you receive each month.

## If You Are Under Age 65

Social Security would prefer that you wait until you are at least age 65 before applying for benefits. Accordingly, if you apply before that age, you will suffer a penalty of reduced benefits beneath the amount of money you would have received if you had waited until age 65. The penalty amounts to approximately a 20 percent cut in the monthly benefit if you apply at age 62. The penalty is a little less for age 63 and 64. This benefit reduction is permanent and will not discontinue upon your reaching age 65.

## If You Are Age 65

This is the age the government considers "normal" for retirement under Social Security law.

## If You Are Over Age 65

The government believes that it saves money if people wait beyond age 65 to apply for benefits. Thus, as an incentive to delay applying, you are "rewarded" with higher benefits for waiting beyond age 65 to join the program. Benefits cease to increase at age 70, so when you reach that age, there is no reason to delay applying for your Social Security retirement benefits – unless you would prefer not to receive your duly-earned benefits.

During your working years, you paid FICA taxes on all of your earned income up to a maximum set by law (currently around $57,600). Just as there is a cap on FICA taxes that can be collected by the government (although the cap may be scrapped to help balance the budget), so too is there a cap on benefits that can be paid to a person age 65 and applying for benefits, currently hovering around $1,128 a month in 1993.

There used to be a "minimum benefits rule," which set a floor on the amount of benefits, since many people earned very low wages in the Depression and War years. That rule is no longer in effect for new applicants.

There is another rule, however, which can help you substantially increase your benefits if you earned low wages over an extended period during your working years. Known as the *Over 10 Rule*, it gives you a chance to receive a higher monthly benefit than you would receive basing your benefit strictly on your earnings history.

Here's how the Over 10 Rule works: For each year you worked in excess of ten years, you will receive a specific dollar benefit, the amount of which is set by law. This dollar figure is multiplied by the number of years you worked over 10. If your regular benefit based on your earnings is disappointing because you had a low earnings history, the Over 10 Rule may help you achieve a higher monthly check.

---

Otto earned low wages his entire working life. Based on the number of years he worked, his earnings and the age at which he applied for Social Security, his monthly check was only $185.

Oscar also earned low wages his entire working life. Under the usual formula, his monthly benefit would also have been $185. Only Oscar knew about the Over 10 Rule and so he asked his Social Security case worker if he qualified. Upon learning that he had 30 years of work under his belt, the worker told Oscar that he did qualify. The formula used that year by Social Security was $18 times the number of years worked, over 10. Oscar nearly doubled his benefit, receiving $360 per month instead of the $185. ($18 x 20 [years] = $360.)

---

## SURVIVORS' BENEFITS

The government also created a Social Security benefit to help provide for the surviving spouse and children of deceased workers. These potential beneficiaries are called survivors. To be considered a survivor for Social Security purposes, at least two things must happen:

- The deceased person must have earned sufficient work credits. For survivors' benefits, the number of work credits required are often fewer than are needed for retirement benefits.

- You must qualify based on your relationship to the deceased: Only spouses, children, and in limited circumstances, parents, qualify.

If you believe you may be entitled to survivors' benefits, here are some of the more important rules you should know about:

- You cannot collect *both* survivors' benefits and your individual benefits. If your own retirement benefits, based on your personal work and income history, would be higher than the survivors' benefits you would receive, you should apply for retirement benefits in your own name. You cannot collect both your individual benefits and survivors' benefits.
- The standard benefit of a surviving spouse of a retired worker is 100 percent of the deceased spouse's benefit. However you must wait until you are age 65 to begin collecting in order to receive the full benefit.
- If you're a surviving spouse you can begin to collect benefits at age 60. You don't have to wait until age 62. However, if you apply at age 60, you will only receive 71.5 percent of the full age 65 benefit. If you begin collecting at 62, the benefit will be about 82.9 percent of the age 65 benefit.
- You can collect if you're a divorced spouse: If you are divorced, you are eligible to claim survivors' benefits if your marriage lasted 10 years or longer with your former spouse who has died. (If there was an intervening marriage which has since ended, you may still qualify.)
- If you're disabled, you're eligible to collect benefits beginning at age 50. To be considered disabled, you must not be able to perform *any* gainful activity. That means you cannot do any work, even the lowest paid or easiest to perform. That is a very tough standard to meet. (If you are disabled and you qualify based on your own work history, you may instead choose to collect Social Security Disability benefits. See below.)
- Parents of a worker may be able to collect benefits. In order to qualify, you must have been dependent for at

least half of the cost of your support, on your working child, based on your earnings and expenses.

- If you are a widow and remarry, you don't lose benefits. Once you begin collecting dependents' benefits, you don't lose them because you remarry.

- You may be able to receive benefits because you are a parent of a minor child. If you are a parent under age 60 and are caring for a dependent child under the age of 16 of your deceased spouse, you can receive survivors' benefits.

- Children of deceased workers can collect benefits. Unmarried children under age 18 (or who are disabled before age 22) can collect benefits if their deceased parent had earned sufficient work quarters or credits to qualify for the benefit.

---

Oscar married Darla, a 35-year-old woman. They had a son named Junior. Oscar died when Junior was 10. Both Darla and her son qualified for survivors' benefits. Darla received benefits until her son turned 16. Junior received benefits until he was 18.

---

## DEPENDENTS' BENEFITS

Social Security also pays benefits to "dependents" under certain conditions. (This is different from survivors' benefits, since dependents' benefits are paid when the worker has not died.) Most people think of a dependent as someone who must, in fact, rely on another for their care and support. But under Social Security, the *fact* of dependency is not what counts. What matters is whether you come under one of the categories permitting you to receive benefits under the dependents program.

In order for dependent benefits to be payable, the worker whose work quarters they are based on must be *eligible* either for retirement benefits or disability benefits. The worker need not actually be receiving the benefits. The following people are considered dependents for purposes of Social Security dependents' benefits:

## A Spouse Age 62 or Older

The benefit payable is generally 50 percent of the worker's rate of benefit earned at age 65. However, the amount of the benefit can be reduced if:

- The worker retires before age 65;
- The spouse applies for benefits before age 65; or
- The worker is receiving Social Security benefits and has benefits reduced due to excess income.

---

Otto began receiving Social Security benefits at age 65. His benefit was $900 per month. Otto's wife, Orinda, had been a homemaker their whole marriage and, except for a brief period during World War II, did not work outside the home. As a result, Orinda did not qualify for Social Security in her own right. At age 65, she applied for benefits as a dependent and received $450 per month.

Oscar retired at age 65. His wife Olanda, had worked throughout their marriage and earned a good wage. At age 65, she applied for benefits based on her own work record and received higher payments than she would have received under Social Security dependents' benefits.

---

## A Spouse Under 62, If Caring for Your Child

The child must be under age 16 or must have been disabled before age 22 for benefits to be paid.

## A Divorced Spouse

The marriage must have lasted 10 years and the worker must be *eligible* for retirement benefits. However, he or she does not have to have applied for retirement benefits for the former spouse to receive dependents' benefits.

## Unmarried Children Under 18

Your children can receive benefits as dependents, in addition to your spouse.

## Unmarried Disabled Children (Any Age)

Your child's disability must have started before age 22.

---

Otto had a child, Otto Jr., when he was 50. When he turned 65, he retired and began to collect benefits. His wife, Orinda, stayed home and cared for junior. When Otto retired, Orinda also applied for dependents benefits and received them until junior turned 16. Junior also applied for benefits when Otto retired and received them until he was 18.

Oscar had a child who was born severely disabled. The boy received dependents' benefits from the day Oscar retired. When Oscar died, he received survivors' benefits.

---

## Grandchildren

Grandchildren may be able to qualify if they actually live with and are cared for by the worker *and* are factually dependent on the grandparent-worker for the cost of their care.

# DISABILITY BENEFITS

Social Security also pays benefits to workers who become disabled and thus cannot earn their own living. Eligibility depends on sufficient work quarters (the number will vary depending on your age) and the nature of your disability.

Different disability insurance plans have differing definitions of the term "disability." For example, your private disability policy may define disability as occurring when you are unable to pursue your *usual occupation* because of injury or disease. Social Security has a much tougher standard. You are only considered disabled and thus potentially qualified for benefits, if you cannot do any substantially gainful work. In other words, you're incapable of working.

The Social Security Administration has a list of conditions it considers disabling. Among them, are the following:

- Diseases of the heart, lung or blood vessels which have resulted in a serious loss of organ function as shown by medical tests
- Severe arthritis causing a substantial inability to use your hands or to walk
- Mental illness resulting in a deterioration in your ability to function in the work place and which seriously impairs your ability to get along with people
- Damage to your brain which has resulted in a severe loss of judgment, intellect or memory
- Cancer which is progressive and has not been controlled
- The loss of major function of both arms, both legs or a leg and an arm
- Diseases of the digestive system which result in severe malnutrition, weakness and anemia
- Serious loss of kidney function
- The total inability to speak

If your condition is not on the list, you must prove that the condition keeps you from earning a substantial living. Cases in Social Security law are full of court interpretations of terms such as "serious loss of function," "serious impairment of the ability to earn," and other similar legal concepts. Your Social Security representative should be able to tell you about the SSA's interpretations and these court rulings. You may also wish to consult with a law school, legal clinic or an attorney, for help receiving these important benefits.

There is a time requirement you must pass before you are eligible. Your disability must be long-term to qualify for benefits. The law requires that your disability will last or has lasted 12 months or is expected to lead to death. There is also a waiting period before you can collect benefits, usually 5 months of continuous disability.

If you collect other benefits for your disability, such as through a state disability insurance plan, your Social Security will not be cut unless the total benefits you receive exceed 80 percent of your usual employment earnings. (However, many private insurance disability policies will cut their payments to you if you also receive Social Security disability benefits.)

If you are disabled, widowed, and you are age 50 or over, you may receive benefits even if you don't personally have sufficient work credits or quarters. However, your deceased spouse must have had sufficient work credits and your disability must have begun within seven years of your spouse's death. If you have any questions about this special qualification program, contact your local Social Security office.

If you have received Social Security disability benefits for 24 months (they don't have to be consecutive months), you are eligible to apply for Medicare, even if you are not age 65. (See Chapters 1-3 for information on Medicare.)

## DEATH BENEFITS

There is a small Social Security death benefit payable to help defray the cost of funeral expenses. The claim must be made within two years of the death of the covered worker. Eligibility is restricted to a spouse who was living with the worker at the time of death, or a spouse or child who would have been eligible for survivors' benefits. The sum payable is quite modest ($255 in 1993). The deceased worker has to have been entitled to Social Security benefits for survivors to collect.

## SUPPLEMENTAL SECURITY INCOME

Supplemental Security Income (SSI) guarantees a minimum income level for the elderly, blind and disabled who are living in poverty. The program is administered through the Social Security Administration, although, like Medicaid, it is jointly financed by the federal government and the states.

In order to qualify for SSI, you have to be virtually destitute. Your earnings must be beneath the poverty level (as defined in your state) and you cannot own any substantial property. (Generally you cannot have property worth more than $3,000 if you are a couple or $2,000 if you are single.) However, like Medicaid, your home and car are usually exempt from being counted in determining your eligibility.

Here are some of the more important rules of SSI that you need to know:

- You have to be age 65, blind or disabled to qualify for SSI.
- There is no quarters of coverage (or work credit) qualification requirement.
- All forms of income, pensions, Social Security, gifts, rents, interest on savings, etc., are counted when determining eligibility.

There are *income exemptions* that may allow you to qualify, even if you seem to have earnings in excess of the maximum permitted. They include:

- The first $20 per month of income you receive from any source except public assistance
- The first $65 of earned income
- Irregular unearned income up to $20 per month
- Food stamps or housing assistance run by a government agency
- Income tax refunds
- Wages received by "volunteer" programs, such as Foster Grandparents and the Senior Companion Program

If you live in a public institution, such as a Veterans' Hospital, you cannot receive SSI (however, you can receive Social Security benefits).

Payments amounts will vary from state-to-state. In 1993, the basic federal benefit was $434 for an individual and $652 for a couple. Many states allow benefits in excess of that amount.

Your payments will be reduced by $1 for every $2 you earn over $65 per month and your benefit will be reduced dollar for dollar for all unearned income over $20 per month. Finally, your benefits can be reduced if you live with a relative or friend and receive *in kind* support, such as food or clothing.

You apply for benefits through your local Social Security office. If you're denied benefits you believe you are entitled to, you can appeal. The appeals process is virtually identical to appeals of Social Security (see Chapter 8).

# 10

# PENSIONS & IRAs

This chapter highlights information you need to know about pensions and *individual retirement savings accounts*, called IRAs. This is important material. Social Security is usually insufficient to meet the financial needs of most seniors and, knowledge being power, the more you know about the rules of these financial programs, the better off you will be. This is true whether you are planning for your retirement or if you have already said *adios* to the old rat race, and need information to help you manage your retirement income.

## PENSIONS

You don't need a book to tell you that pensions are important. Receiving a pension can make the difference between an enjoyable and comfortable retirement, where you can afford to pursue the enjoyable things in life such as travel and hobbies, or living on the edge of financial insecurity with the wolf baying at your door. Pensions truly have the power to transform your retirement time into "golden years."

Pensions generally fall into two types: defined benefit and defined contribution plans.

## Defined Benefit Plans

The *defined benefit* plan is probably the most common pension system and it is the easiest one to understand. Basically, in a defined benefit pension, you are guaranteed a specific amount when you retire. The amount can be a specified dollar amount per month for each year of service to your company or union or your pension can be paid based on a specified percentage of your average salary over the years. Whichever it is, the amount of your pension is based on a set formula, hence the term, defined benefit.

## Defined Contribution Plans

In a *defined contribution* plan type pension, the amount of money you will receive as a pension is not guaranteed. Rather, your employer promises to contribute a specified amount of money per employee into the pension plan itself. This money is then invested by the administrators of the pension fund. When you retire, you are entitled to receive pension payments based on the amount your employer has contributed for your individual benefit plus a proportionate share of the earnings the plan has earned over the years. Because you are not guaranteed a specific amount, you will not know exactly how much you will receive until you retire, at which time, you can usually elect to receive a lump sum payment or receive monthly payments. You can request, at least once a year, an individual benefit statement to find out what your accrued benefit is to date. (If you employer only guarantees to contribute a percentage of the company's profits, it is called a profit-sharing plan.)

# TYPICAL RETIREMENT SYSTEMS

There are various retirement systems, including the private, civil service and railroad retirement pension systems.

## Private Pension Systems

Private pension systems cover individuals in companies or union-sponsored plans. Private pensions are regulated by the federal law known as *Employee Retirement Income Security Act* (ERISA). ERISA establishes individual rights under pension plans and investment rules for plan officials.

## Civil Service Pension Systems

If you work for a government entity, you probably will have some substantial pension benefits. While government pensions vary, benefits are generally based on the number of years you were employed and an average of a specified number of your *highest* earning years. For example, the federal government computes the average based on the retiree's three highest years of salary. Civil service pensions often include:

- Cost of Living Adjustments
- Rights to receive your pension upon retirement after only five years on the job (some private pensions require longer periods, such as union-sponsored pension plans)

The one drawback to a civil service pension is that money collected under the system may be considered earned income by Social Security, which can reduce your Social Security retirement benefits.

## Railroad Retirement Pension System

This system, unique to railroad workers, is similar to Social Security in its operation. If you have any questions, contact the Railroad Retirement System at: 844 N. Rush St., Chicago, IL, 60611, or call: (312) 751-4500.

# VESTING

In order to collect pension dollars, you must be *vested* in the program, meaning you must meet the plan's requirements necessary to give you the legal right to receive your pension benefits. The specific vesting rules for your plan will be set forth in the terms of your retirement plan, which will be summarized in your "summary plan description" booklet. Vesting rules usually involve spending a specified number of years on the job. Most plans give you a year of vesting credit if you work at least 1,000 hours during a plan year. Other plans look at the annual date of employment when determining whether or not you earned a year of credit. To find out when your plan year begins, check your plan booklet.

Vesting can be total, meaning you are entitled to receive 100 percent of the pension benefits, or partial, meaning you receive a percentage of benefits. If you leave the job or retire before you have vested, you will receive no benefits.

It is important that you understand the rules of vesting before deciding whether to retire, quit your job or change positions. Ask your employer or plan administrator to explain the vesting rules for your retirement plan.

Under law, employers are able to take into consideration the amount of Social Security you collect in determining what your pension benefit will be. If your employer adopts this method, it will probably be an integrated plan.

## Integrated Plans

Some pension plans offer less than they seem to promise on the surface. These are called *integrated plans.* Integrated pension plans boast that they will guarantee you a certain percentage of your working monthly income when you retire. The level promised is called the goal. Here's the catch. Your pension will be integrated with your Social Security to achieve the goal. That often means *your pension will pay you less per month than you would have been paid without the integration clause.*

Otto had an integrated pension plan. His plan set a goal of $1,200 in combined private pension money and Social Security per month in Otto's pocket upon retirement. Under the terms of his pension plan, Otto had "earned" $700 per month. However, Otto received $750 a month in Social Security when he retired. That would have amounted to a $1,450 per month income, $250 more than his $1,200 goal. Because his pension was integrated, his private pension was legally allowed to reduce its payment by $250, thereby meeting the integrated goal of $1,200.

## HOW TO RECEIVE YOUR BENEFITS

Many plans give you several options about how you can receive your pension benefits. The specific terms governing these choices will be set forth in your pension plan.

Your available choices will generally be broken down into the following options:

### Lump Sum or Monthly Payment?

Defined contribution plans allow you to choose a large, one-time-only lump-sum payment or periodic payments for the rest of your life. There are pros and cons to either option. Taking your money in a lump-sum payment is tantalizing because the sum is often quite large. In addition, by accepting your pension all at once, you are guaranteed to receive all of the pension money you are entitled to, while if you take a monthly benefit and die young you may receive less than your full due. On the other hand, if you take a lump sum and spend it or invest it unwisely, it is gone forever. Two other important points: Most plans require you to submit a signed, notarized statement from your spouse if you plan to accept a lump-sum, and accepting a large sum at one time can have a significant income tax consequence. Thus, before deciding how to receive your money and whether you can defer the tax, consult your C.P.A. or attorney.

## Should Spouse Receive Payments After You Die?

If you take your pension in monthly or other periodic increments, your pension payments usually cease if you die. However, plans generally allow you to provide for payments to your spouse after your death unless you and your spouse agree otherwise in a notarized written statement. If you decide against a lump-sum payment, you will accept a lower periodic payment. If your spouse seems likely to outlive you and doesn't have pension benefits, this may be the best way to go.

## Does the Plan Offer Early Retirement?

In this troubled economy, many companies are laying off workers and permanently down-sizing. Under these conditions, many may want to take (or be forced to take) early retirement. Many plans pay benefits for vested employees who take early retirement. The quid pro quo for early retirement is usually a lower benefit. However, unlike Social Security, private pension early retirement plans allow you to begin to receive benefits when you are relatively young – say at age 55 – allowing you the security of a guaranteed income while you pursue new projects, perhaps as an entrepreneur, an employee in a new career or as a semi-retired part-time worker who is able to concentrate on hobbies.

## Are There Other Benefits Available to You?

Some plans offer continuing health and life insurance benefits as part of retirement or discount the premiums for continued coverage. Others continue to allow retirees to use credit unions and discount purchasing services. These perquisites can be of great value to you and should be thoroughly understood before you retire.

## FEDERAL LAW AND YOUR PENSION

As previously mentioned, private pensions are governed by the federal law called the Employee Retirement Income Security Act (ERISA), which, along with other federal statutes, protect your pension rights. Here are some of the more important protections afforded by the law:

### Information About Your Pension Is Available

You cannot fully understand your pension unless given the information necessary to understand how it operates. ERISA establishes your right to ask for and receive a "Summary Plan Description," which will describe:

- How your plan works
- Your options for collecting benefits
- The rules of participation
- How your benefits accrue
- How your rights vest
- Your choices for other benefits
- Your right to request an individual benefit's statement – contact your plan administrator for further details

### Annual Reports Must Be Made to the Government

ERISA requires each plan governed by the law to make a yearly report to the government about the financial investments of the plan. You have a right to receive a copy of this annual financial report which discloses how much money is in the pension and how it's being invested. The report is referred to as the IRS Form 5500 – again, ask your plan administrator.

### The Law Protects Your Accrued Pension Credits

At one time, an extensive illness or work lay-off could have led to the loss of your accrued pension benefits, interfering with your ability to vest. Federal law now protects accrued benefits. Called the *break in service rules,* under the law you cannot lose your accrued pension credits unless you are off from work for five or more years.

> Oscar worked for Wally's Widget Conglomerate, Incorporated. He worked for two years, accruing pension rights under the Wally's Pension Plan as he went along. A recession hit and Wally's Widget was forced to lay off Oscar for one year. When Oscar was brought back to work the boss at Wally's told Oscar that he had lost all of his pension credits. But Oscar knew that under the law, he could not have his accrued pension credits taken from him unless he had been out of work for five or more years. He pointed out the law to his employer and soon had all of his pension credits restored.

## Your Vesting Rights Cannot Be Changed

Once you have your rights vested under an existing plan, they cannot be withdrawn or reduced by a change in the vesting rules of your plan.

## The Pension Benefit Guaranty Corporation

Pension funds are generally well-managed and financially healthy. However, some funds have been known to go broke. If yours is one of the unfortunate (or mismanaged) ones, what then? Do you lose all of your pension? Maybe yes and maybe no. The ERISA statute created the Pension Benefit Guaranty Corporation (PBGC), a government agency that provides an insurance safety net when a plan paying fixed benefits stops because it lacks the money to pay promised pensions. The PBGC is a good thing, but its benefits are limited:

- The PBGC insures only against bankruptcy for defined benefit pension plans. It does *not* provide protection against the failure of defined contribution plans.

- The PBGC may not protect all of your monetary pension, if your benefits are substantial.
- The PBGC does not guarantee all of the benefits you may be owed. For example, unvested rights are not protected, nor are nonmonetary benefits, such as extended health insurance coverage.
- There is an on-going controversy that the fund is not well financed and a major pension plan failure could bankrupt the program.

If you have any questions about the Pension Benefit Guaranty Corporation, write to PBGC, 2020 K St., N.W., Washington, D.C. 20006, or call (202) 788-8800.

## ENFORCING YOUR RIGHTS

Under ERISA, you can file suit in Federal District Court to enforce your rights. However, it is advised that you exhaust the pension plan's administrative appeals process prior to filing suit, since many courts require that initial step. In court, you are entitled to recover benefits you were improperly denied, seek to have an unfair rule regarding future rights reversed or changed, correct improper management of your pension plan or otherwise enforce your ERISA guaranteed rights. Also, under ERISA, you may be able to have some or all of your attorney's fees paid if you win the case.

### Tax Issues

Pension benefits which you receive are taxable as you collect them. However, there are portions of your pension that may be exempt from taxation. These include:

- Benefits attributable to your own *after-tax contributions* will not be taxed again. In other words, if you paid extra money into the plan from your net paycheck, that money will not be subject to a second tax.

- If the payment is considered an annuity, some of the money may not be taxable (see Chapter 11).
- Some of a long-term pension received in lump sum may be treated as five-year averaging.

The issue of pensions and taxation is a complicated one, where "I-dots" and "T-crosses" really matter. Thus, it is important you consult a financial advisor or tax specialist before making any decisions involving substantial funds with regard to your pension or your tax status.

## INDIVIDUAL RETIREMENT ACCOUNTS

Individual Retirement Accounts (IRAs) are a relatively new retirement investment device, first appearing on the financial scene in 1974. IRAs were and are intended to promote savings and, at the same time, help working men and women prepare for their retirement. They are, in essence, tax shelters for the middle class.

If you open an IRA account, you can deposit $2,000 or 100 percent of your earned income, whichever is less, per year into the account, and you *may* be able to deduct the amount you invested from your income when computing your federal and state income taxes. You can deduct the entire amount of your contribution if you're single and not participating in any other retirement plan.

However, if you participate in another retirement plan, such as a pension plan, 401K annuity or Keogh, then the deductibility of your contribution depends on your adjusted gross income. In 1993, if you participated in another retirement plan and earned less than $25,000, your contribution was fully deductible. If you earned between $25,000 and $30,000, a partial deduction was allowed and if you earned over $30,000, none of your contribution was deductible.

Your marital status can also effect the deductibility of your contribution. If you're married and you or your spouse participates in another retirement plan, the government considers both of you covered by that plan. Again, your

IRA deduction could be reduced or eliminated, depending on your adjusted gross income.

Unlike standard bank accounts or certificates of deposit, the interest you earn in the IRA account is tax-deferred. That means you will not have to pay a tax on the interest as it accrues. (You will also probably earn a higher rate of interest because the account is long-term.)

When you withdraw money from your IRA, you will pay federal and state income tax on the proceeds you take out. If you withdraw money before you reach age 59 1/2, you will also have to pay a 10 percent tax penalty, and in addition, there may be a state income tax penalty as well. You can begin to withdraw your money without penalty at age 59 1/2. You must begin to withdraw your money at age 70 1/2.

The rules of IRAs are continually subject to change based on the politics of the moment. So, before you take any major step regarding your IRA, be sure to consult the IRS, your tax advisor or an official of a bank or other savings institution who is knowledgeable about IRA matters.

# *11*

# LIFE INSURANCE
# & ANNUITIES

Many seniors were avid purchasers of life insurance in the post-war years. And why not? As parents, you deeply believed that protecting your family from the financial cost of the death of the bread winner was a top priority. This was especially important in that era where one-income households were the rule, not the exception. You may have also purchased life insurance as an investment, so that over the years the policy would accrue sufficient value to send your kids to college or to help pay for your retirement.

Now that you are in your harvest years, what is the role of life insurance during your retirement? (For the purposes of our discussion, it is assumed you have life insurance currently in effect.) Should you cash in your existing policy? Can it be a source of income to you? What are the tax considerations? This chapter discusses the role of life insurance in your life as a senior citizen and the considerations of cashing in your policy. We will also take a brief look at investment policies, known as annuities.

## LIFE INSURANCE

There are two broad categories of life insurance: term life insurance and cash value life insurance. The sole purpose of term insurance is to pay benefits if and when the person covered by the policy dies. The policy itself is not worth any money. If you cancel the policy, the premiums you paid are gone forever. Term life insurance policies are in effect only during the "term" of the policy; that is, the length the policy is in effect. Term policies tend to be quite expensive in the senior years because the likelihood of dying is much higher than it is for a healthy younger person, who as a consequence, pays a smaller premium.

Cash value policies (also known as whole life, universal life, etc.) on the other hand, accrue value over the life of the policy. You pay more in early years so the cash value can accrue. (That is one of the reasons cash value life insurance premiums generally cost more than term life insurance premiums.) Your company then invests and manages the surplus money and you achieve a return, which will vary from policy to policy. Company profits and agent commissions tend to be higher with cash value policies.

The amount of the cash that accrues in a policy varies from policy to policy, depending on the size of the premium, the interest or earnings that the company applies to the policy, the length of the policy, the amount of commission and other costs charged by the life insurance company, and other factors.

Life insurance provides one of the few middle-class tax advantages left after the tax reform laws of the 1980s. Most of the tax breaks are for those who own cash value policies, although term life insurance beneficiaries receive some tax benefits, too. Among the tax benefits and considerations available to you as the owner or beneficiary of a life insurance policy are the following:

### The Policy's Increasing Value Is Tax Deferred

If you have a bank account, you know that the interest you earn each year is taxed by the government. Not so with the cash value you accrue each year in your life insurance policy. It is tax-deferred, so long as you do not cash in the policy.

### There May Be Tax Considerations If Cashed-In

If you own a cash value policy that has an accrued value, you can cancel your policy and have the accrued value plus any dividends you may have received paid to you by the life insurance company. When you receive this money, it is *not* subject to income tax, unless the cash value plus any policy dividends you may have received exceed the sum of the premiums you have paid. However, you can deduct the amount of the premiums you paid over the life of the policy which will reduce or could even eliminate the tax bite.

### You Can Borrow Against the Policy Without Paying Taxes

If you need money and are thinking of cashing in your life insurance policy, think first about borrowing against the cash value. The right to borrow against the value of a policy is one real benefit of owning a life insurance policy with cash value. Here's why. When you borrow against the value (which you own) you can receive the money and not pay income taxes on it. You pay taxes only if the cash value plus any dividends you may have received exceed the sum of the premiums you have paid. If you die and the loan hasn't been paid, the amount owed plus interest will be deducted from the death proceeds paid to your beneficiary. The IRS has some specific rules to prevent abuse, so be sure to discuss this issue with your agent, or consult your accountant or the IRS.

### Life Insurance Proceeds Are Usually Not Taxed

Life insurance proceeds paid upon the death of the insured are generally not subject to state and federal income tax. However, proceeds may be subject to an estate tax.

Wealthier people often use life insurance trusts as a tool of estate planning to avoid *probate* expenses. If you have any questions about using life insurance in this manner, consult with a life insurance agent or an estate planning professional.

## LIFE INSURANCE FOR SENIORS

In recent years, a growing number of life insurance companies have focused on selling term life insurance to senior citizens. Most of these policies are sold by mail. Many are advertised on television, using phrases such as "No medical exam required," "Think of it, term life insurance for only $4.95 per month!" and, "You can't be turned down for any reason."

These policies are perfectly legal. But beware. They often offer much less than you might think from the sales pitch. Watch out for:

- Life insurance that is sold in units of coverage: One unit rarely buys much coverage and most of these policies seldom permit you to buy more than 5–10 thousand dollars' worth of insurance at anywhere near an affordable price. Usually, the policies aren't worth that much.
- Policies that have long waiting periods before going into effect.
- Policies that require the bulk of the benefits to be payable only upon accidental death. If you die during the waiting period, the only money your beneficiary usually receives is a return of the premiums paid before your death.
- Natural death benefits that may only be in the hundreds of dollars. Often these so called life insurance policies are accidental death policies that only pay a lesser amount when death occurs as a result of natural causes.
- Benefits that are reduced as you age.

Whether to buy one of these policies is up to you. Don't do it because of the sales pitch but on the basis of providing for a valid need, such as paying for a funeral. And before you sign on the dotted line, take the time to read the fine print. You may decide the policy just isn't worth the money you will be paying in premiums.

# ANNUITIES

It is important to differentiate between life insurance and annuities. They are quite different. Life insurance is primarily designed to pay money benefits on the death of the insured. Annuities, on the other hand, are usually designed to provide an income for the policy holder's later years. Frequently, but not always, the two policies are sold by the same companies.

When you buy an annuity you pay an agreed upon amount of money to the annuity company, which invests it and in return, guarantees you an income over a specified term, or for the duration of your life, depending on the terms of the annuity contract. Benefit payments are usually made monthly, quarterly, yearly or in a lump sum.

The amount of your payments are determined by the amount of the premium you paid and the interest the annuity earns and the time it was held by the company before making payments to you. The annuity payments can begin immediately, but most people defer receiving money until a later time, typically to about the time of retirement. If payments are deferred, the interest credited to your contract builds up free of current income tax. Once you start to receive a monthly payment, the government begins to tax the accumulated interest. Part of each payment will be interest and will be taxed as ordinary income. The other part is principal and is not taxable. This is true of both deferred and immediate annuities.

If you have further questions about your life insurance policy or annuities, contact your State Department of Insurance and ask if they have a consumers' guide to send, and of course, your insurance agent. You can also contact the National Insurance Consumer Helpline, toll free at

(800) 942-4242. While they do not provide company specific information, they do answer general questions and provide brochures upon request.

# 12

## TAPPING YOUR HOME FOR INCOME

You may be one of the many senior citizens in this country who is property rich but cash poor. For example, you may own your own house outright or have a tremendous amount of equity in it (the difference between what is owed and what the property is worth). At the same time, your monthly income may be restricted to Social Security and a small pension. That may leave you in the uncomfortable position of having insufficient cash to pay your bills or to enjoy the many recreational opportunities that can make life worth living.

### THE REVERSE MORTGAGE

At one time, if you wanted to take cash out of the equity in your home, your choices would have been limited to selling it or borrowing money through a conventional mortgage. Both choices have their drawbacks. If you sell, you have to find a new place to live, and you may have to pay a capital gains tax on the increase in value of the property over what you invested in it (subject to a one-time-only $125,000 exemption for senior citizens). Borrowing against the income in your house would substantially increase your monthly expenses and create the danger of foreclosure if you ran into money troubles. Now, there's another choice. It is called a home equity conversion, more commonly known as the *reverse mortgage*.

A reverse mortgage is a loan on the equity in your home. However, rather than receive the money in a large lump sum and then have to pay a large loan payment back to the bank each month, you receive monthly payments, which you don't repay during your lifetime as long as you don't move to a new home.

If you are interested in the reverse mortgage, here are some facts you need to know about it:

- You receive monthly or periodic payments. Instead of receiving your money in a lump sum, you receive a monthly check.
- Each payment you receive increases the amount that is owed on the house. Thus, instead of the loan shrinking with each payment you make, it increases with each payment you receive.
- The amount you receive will depend on your equity, the interest rate charged and the length of the loan contract. If you have a lot of equity, you can receive higher payments than if you have relatively low equity. Also, the length of the contract and interest rate will affect the amount you receive.
- You have the right to stay in your home. You do not lose ownership of your home. You can remain in your home while you receive your money.
- The debt does not have to be repaid until you die or permanently leave your home. When you die, the money you received will be owed back to the lending institution, plus accrued interest. The same is true if you permanently move out of your home or sell it. Many reverse mortgages contain terms protecting your property if you have an extended stay in a nursing home.
- Because the money is a loan, there is no income tax owed: That increases the buying power of the money you receive.

There are some disadvantages to a reverse mortgage that you should explore thoroughly before making a decision:

- Depending on the terms of the agreement, your home could become the property of the lender upon your death: Should you die before your life expectancy, you would have received less money than the house was worth. Moreover, there would be nothing remaining of the property to leave to your heirs.
- There are closing costs associated with reverse mortgages. If you live long enough, much or all of your equity may be lost to your heirs. Also, the cost of a reverse mortgage will probably be higher than a standard property-secured loan.
- If you are on SSI or Medicaid, the proceeds you receive may cause you to lose your eligibility: While your home is exempt from being counted against you, loan proceeds may count as "income."

Reverse mortgage contracts are usually complicated documents filled with legalese and fine print provisions which can have a material impact on your finances and estate. It is vital to your financial health and peace of mind that you take the time and care to understand all of the contract terms. Ask questions of the proposed lender. Find out about the law (many states have passed laws governing reverse mortgages). Think about the possible worst case scenario by asking yourself, "What if?" If you have any questions about any term or provision, ask them and get the answer in writing so that you have proof of the information given you before signing the contract. Remember the old adage, "Everything is negotiable." Don't be afraid to object to a term or provision you don't want to agree to and don't sign a reverse mortgage contract you do not believe gives you a fair deal.

## THE LEASE-BACK SALE

Somewhat akin to the reverse mortgage, and another way to convert your real estate into cash while remaining in your home is the lease-back sale. As the name implies, the lease-back involves a sale of your property with your right to lease it back from the new owner guaranteed in the contract of purchase.

Here's the way the lease-back usually works: You sell your house to a person or business entity. You're given the right to live in the property for the rest of your life. This is usually accomplished by setting the length of the lease in excess of your reasonable life expectancy. You receive a lump-sum or monthly payments as the sale price and you pay rent back to the owner (now your landlord). The rent you pay is usually less than the income you receive, giving you extra money in your pocket each month. Or, if you receive a lump sum, you can invest the money you receive to earn an income. (However, with interest so low these days, that may not be very much money.) Another plus: The major repairs, taxes and insurance are now your landlord's responsibility, so your expenses may be reduced.

At one time, many parents and adult children entered into a lease-back arrangement in order to avoid probate and to give the children a good tax break. However, the Tax Reform Act of 1986 dealt a blow to such family arrangements when it limited the deductions available on rental properties.

## SELLING YOUR HOUSE

Many seniors get money for their retirement years by selling their home, taking the one-time-only capital gains tax exclusion, and investing the money they receive from the sale to produce an income.

This step should be considered long and hard before putting the "For Sale" sign up on the front lawn. Selling your home involves many legal, financial and emotional decisions. Property values are, as of this writing, depressed in many areas and interest rates have fallen so low that the income that could be derived from the proceeds of a sale may not be worth the loss of a piece of real property that is substantially or completely paid for.

If you decide to sell your house you may wish to hire a real estate agent. If you do, be sure to take the following steps:

## Shop Around

Interview several agents for the "job" and select the one whose combination of training, experience and personality seem best suited to your needs.

## Check the Agent's Training and Expertise

You want a dedicated professional as your agent, not one who works in his or her spare time.

## Negotiate the Commission

The real estate profession is very competitive. Use this fact to your advantage to get a favorable commission (the percentage of the sale the real estate agent receives).

## Obtain a Copy of the NBR's Code of Ethics

If your realtor is a member of the National Board of Realtors (most are), he or she will have a copy to give you.

# PART 3

# MISCELLANEOUS SENIOR SERVICES & LEGAL RIGHTS

*13*

# PROBATE &
# ESTATE PLANNING

As people grow older and death becomes more than an abstract concept, their minds and hearts turn increasingly to providing for their loved ones who are left behind. Who do they want to own their home? How much money do they want to leave to their children or grandchildren? To whom do they want to give precious family heirlooms? Are there bequests to charities they wish to make after they are gone?

The state cares about after-death matters too, although in a far less sentimental way. The government's interest is in an orderly and peaceful transfer of property from the dead to the living, the payment of the deceased's debts and the collection of taxes. The legal process by which this is done is called probate. Planning ahead for probate (or to avoid it) is called estate planning.

## HOW PROBATE WORKS

Probate is a legal action governed by the laws of each state. Probate takes place in Probate Court, where the court reviews the circumstances of the estate and issues orders about its distribution consistent with state law. The purpose of a probate is to legally transfer property, either as instructed in your will or as mandated by state law, if there is no legally valid will. Probate also allows creditors to petition for the payment of debts. Final taxes are also levied and ordered paid during the probate process. In short, probate brings finality to all of the legal and business affairs of the deceased.

This is all well and good but there's a catch. Probating an estate can cost the estate a lot of money. Attorneys may be retained and may be paid from estate assets based on a percentage of the appraised value, and they may charge extra money if they do work above and beyond the usual paper shuffling. (For example, a lawyer supervising the sale of real property in a probate case can charge an extra fee.) That is one reason there is a growing consumer movement toward "do-it-yourself" probates and movements to limit attorneys fees to hourly rates.

In addition, the person or business entity named to administer the descendant's estate during probate, usually called an *executor*, also can charge the estate for their services. To add insult to financial injury, many states also tax the estate based on its monetary worth. If the taxable estate exceeds $600,000, the federal government gets into the act and charges a huge inheritance tax. Thus, the higher the value of the estate, the more of it goes to lawyers, executors and tax collectors, and the less goes to family and heirs.

That's where estate planning comes in. At its most basic level, by writing a will, estate planning allows you to direct how and to whom your estate is to be distributed after you die. But estate planning does more than that. If your estate is worth a lot of money, estate planning can do things to lower the value of the estate in the eyes of the law. This, in turn, reduces the amount of taxes owed. Effective estate planning can also lower the amount of legal fees involved. Some methods of estate planning have been created so that they eliminate the need for probate altogether. You may have heard of the phrase, "avoiding probate."

If you are going to write a will or have been named as an executor or heir in someone else's will, it is important for you to obtain working knowledge of how probate works.*

# WILLS

Everyone needs a will. If you die without one, you lose control over who gets your property. You will be unable to give specific items to specific people since your entire estate will be distributed to your heirs as provided by law.

A will allows you to name who you want to take care of your minor children, will distribute your property and take care of all financial matters. It even allows you to "disinherit" heirs you do not want to give property to.

Each state has its own laws regarding the validity of wills and how they are to be probated. However, the following general principles usually apply:

## A Handwritten Will May Be Legal

Many people write wills in their own hand. These are known as holographic wills. Holographic wills can be legal, even if they are not witnessed, but usually must be *dated*, written entirely in your *own handwriting* and *signed*. Holographic wills are not legal in every state.

## Most States Permit Fill-In-The-Blank Wills

As the legal consumer movement has grown and people have tried to break the monopoly of lawyers over all matters legal, form wills have come into acceptance in most areas of the country. Those of you with smaller estates can take advantage of this type of will with little fear that your wishes will be invalidated. Some states have passed

---

* For step-by-step information on the probate process, see *Probate: Settling An Estate,* by Kay Ostberg in association with HALT, Random House, 1990, $8.95.

laws permitting statutory fill-in-the-blank wills, including CA, WI, and ME. However, don't alter the form in any way, or all bets may be off.

## FORMAL WILLS

For our purposes, a formal will shall be defined as one that is tailor-made to your estate, typed, dated, and signed in front of witnesses who sign a special attestation clause that you signed the will in their presence – as required by the laws of the state in which you reside. Formal wills can be simple, giving all of your assets to your spouse, or may be quite complex, with many built in contingencies and/or the creation of multiple trusts. If you have a lawyer prepare a simple will, the cost is rather modest; usually in the low hundreds for a husband and wife. A complicated will involving multiple trusts, however, can run into the thousands and may be as long as a short book.

Regardless of the type of will you create, there are some facts that are true of all of them:

### You Must Be Competent to Make a Will

If the will is legally challenged (about 4 percent are), it will be invalidated if the court finds that you were not competent when you signed the will. The issue of competence is a legal one, but basically it means you were of sound mind and memory when you created the will and not under duress, menace, fraud or undue influence.

### Only One Will Is Valid at a Time

If you prepare a new will that is executed properly, any previous wills are considered null and void and without legal effect.

### You Can Revoke Your Will at Any time

You can invalidate your will by destroying it, defacing it or otherwise taking action, such as writing a new will.

### You Can Modify a Will

The document that modifies wills is called a *codicil*. A codicil allows you to make minor changes in your will without having to rewrite the entire document. However, the codicil must be typed, dated, signed and witnessed in the same formal manner as your original will was.

### New Family Circumstances Can Affect Your Will

For example, if you marry, divorce or have a child after your will has been signed, it can affect the enforceability of the document.

### If You Don't Have a Legal Will, State Law Applies

If you don't have a legal will when you die, it is called dying *intestate*. When this happens, someone will have to file an action in probate court and seek to establish the right to "administer" the estate. The property is then divided according to state law.

Getting a will drafted doesn't have to be expensive. Low-cost help is available through legal clinics, advocacy groups for the elderly, group legal service plans and lawyers. You can also write your own will through the use of do-it-yourself kits, books or software packages.*

## TRUSTS

---

* For step-by-step instructions on writing a will, see HALT's book, *Wills: A Do-It-Yourself Guide,* by Theresa Meehan Rudy and Jean Dimeo, 1992, $8.95.

A trust is a legal entity that can own, hold and pay out *assets* (money or property) that are given to it. You establish a trust by signing a document that creates the trust entity and then by transferring title of the property you are placing in trust into the trust itself. At that point, you no longer own the property: the trust does.

One of the most important purposes of a trust, when created during your life, is to eliminate or reduce probate expenses. How is this done? By reducing the size of your estate. When you transfer your property into a trust, you don't own it as an individual anymore. The trust does. When you die, the property in trust is not subject to probate (although it may be subject to taxes).

## The Players

The following people or entities are key to understanding trusts:

**The Trustor.** The trustor (sometimes called grantor) is the person making the trust. It is his or her property that goes into the trust and he or she is the one who sets the purposes of the trust and the rules by which the trust will be managed.

**The Trustee.** The trustee is the person or business (such as a bank) that manages the property in the trust and complies with its terms. A trustee is a *fiduciary*, that is, he or she legally owes the highest loyalty to the trust beneficiaries).

**The Beneficiaries.** The beneficiaries are the persons who are to receive the money or otherwise benefit from the trust and for whom it is managed. The beneficiaries can be anyone you name in the trust, including yourself, your children, or a charitable organization.

## The Kinds of Trusts

There are several kinds of trusts:

- Trusts can be created during your life or in a will. A trust created during your life is called an *"inter vivos* or living trust."* If a trust is created in your will to go into effect upon your death, it is called a *testamentary trust.*
- Trusts can be revocable or irrevocable. If you create an "irrevocable trust" you can never cancel it or change it. The property cannot be taken back nor can the purposes of the trust be changed. If you create a "revocable trust," you can cancel the trust, modify its terms or take the property back. There are differences in taxation with regard to the property placed in trust, depending on whether the trust is revocable or irrevocable.

## Even If You Create a Trust, You Need a Will

Trusts can't do everything. For example, a trust does not name a guardian for minor children, nor does it distribute property upon your death that has not actually been placed into the trust itself (for example, if you inherit property shortly before you die).

## Bank Accounts Can Be Held in Trust

This is accomplished by signing a simple form your bank will have for that purpose. Bank accounts held in trust can be transferred to the beneficiaries free of probate.

The most famous trust in estate planning is the living trust. A living trust is designed to remove ownership of your property from you to the trust, so that, when you die, there is nothing to probate.

Otto decided to create a living trust. He went to his lawyer, who prepared the document which Otto signed. The trust cost about $1,000 for his lawyer to prepare in the community where Otto lived. Otto was the trustor, since his property was put into the trust. Otto also made himself the trustee, so that he could continue to manage the property himself. Otto also named himself as the beneficiary of the trust, so he could benefit from the trust property. And he also named his children as alternate beneficiaries; that is, they were to become the beneficiaries of the trust upon his death, after which the trust would end and his children would receive the trust property. When Otto died, there was no probate because he owned no property at his death. The property then went to his children, free and clear of probate costs.

Nothing in life is perfect, and that includes living trusts. A living trust does not prevent the government from taxing the estate, nor does it protect the property against creditors. (The probate process cuts off creditors after the probate is over. A trust does not.) You should also be alert for high-pressured and high-priced offers to prepare a living trust, often by unqualified door-to-door salespeople. The shady practices of a few aggressive and sometimes fraudulent persons should not deter you from considering the possibility of creating a trust.

Trusts are used for many purposes beyond estate planning. For example, a spendthrift trust protects a financially irresponsible beneficiary from the mismanagement of his or her financial affairs, a special needs trust can provide for items not covered under Medicaid, and a childrens' trust can be established to finance your children's education.*

## GIFT GIVING

You don't have to wait until you die to distribute your property. You can give it away. This too can reduce or

---

* For a discussion of the different types of trusts available, see *How to Use Trusts to Avoid Probate & Taxes: A Guide to Living, Marital, Support, Charitable and Insurance Trusts*, by Theresa Meehan Rudy, Kay Ostberg and Jean Dimeo in association with HALT, Random House, 1992, $10.

eliminate costs because property you do not own cannot be subject to probate or taxes when you die. So, if you have property you no longer use or money you want your child or another loved one to have, you can give it to them while you are alive and reduce the size of your estate.

Gift giving has legal consequences that you should understand before you give your property away:

## There May Be a Tax Consequence

If you give away more than $10,000 per year in cash or property to any individual or noncharitable organization, you can be subject to paying a gift tax.

## You Lose Control Over the Property

If the property you give away is a gift, you no longer own it. If you still control the property, it is not a gift and could be part of your estate for tax purposes.

## A Gift Cannot Be Taken Back

A gift transfers title to the property given to the recipient. Once complete, it cannot be revoked.

## Gifts Given Within Three Years of Death May Be Subject to Taxes

The most common example of this is ownership of a life insurance policy.

## Gifts to a Minor Can Get Complicated

Giving to minors is a tricky business because most states require that property held by minors be supervised by an adult. For this reason, property (of any meaningful value) given to minors usually involves the appointment of a guardian, such as a parent or financial institution, who will manage the property on behalf of the minor until he or she reaches 18 or 21 years old – whichever is the age of maturity in the child's state.

## JOINT TENANCY

Joint tenancy is one way in which two or more people can own property. Many seniors use "joint tenancy" to make sure their house, bank account, car, or other assets pass directly to their spouse, child or other person without having to go through probate or be sold. The major legal significance of a joint tenancy is that when one joint tenant dies, his or her share of the property becomes the property of the surviving joint tenant(s), rather than passing to the descendants' heirs. This is called the "right to survivorship."

If you sign a deed making a child or other loved one a joint tenant in your property, no probate will be required and the expense of that legal process will be avoided. The idea is simple: since the ownership of the property at the time of death is legally transferred to the surviving joint tenant, it cannot be subject to probate. (This is one reason many married couples hold their property in joint tenancy.)

Placing property you currently own separately into a joint tenancy may avoid probate but it can have some significant legal drawbacks, including the following:

### You Lose Exclusive Control Over the Property

Joint tenants have the right to equal control over the property. Thus, if you place your property in joint tenancy, your joint tenant has an equal say in managing the property.

> Oscar wanted to avoid probate so he placed his house into joint tenancy with his brother Otto. Later, Oscar wanted to sell the house but Otto refused. Oscar had to sue for the right to sell the property and then only received 50 percent of the net proceeds.

Otto also wanted to avoid probate. He created a living trust, naming Oscar as his alternate beneficiary. He placed his house as an asset of the trust. Thereafter, he decided to sell his house. Since he was the trustee of his own trust, and since Oscar had no legal title to his house, Otto was able to complete the sale without asking Oscar's permission.

## A Joint Tenant Could Force You to Sell the Property

Remember, you no longer own the property but co-own it. That means, your joint tenant can force *you* to sell or buy-out the property you use to own solely in your own name, at any time.

## Creditors May Be Able to Get at the Property

If someone is legally in debt, his or her property can be used to pay off the debt. This may include your joint tenants share of the property.

## You Could Be Subject to a Gift Tax

Just because you give part ownership and not sole ownership of property, that does not mean you have not given a gift.

## Estate Taxes May Not Be Avoided

Again, probate expenses and estate taxes are two different kettles of money. Joint tenancy avoids probate. It may not avoid taxes.

This ends our brief discussion of wills and estate planning. If you want more information, there are many books available which go into more detail; see Appendix 4. Many senior centers also offer seminars and lectures on these topics by estate-planning lawyers, which can be very informative.

# *14*

# GUARDIANSHIPS &
# POWERS OF ATTORNEY

If you are like many senior citizens, you may worry about what will happen if you are temporarily or permanently incapacitated by illness or disease. Who will collect your pension and Social Security? Who will pay your bills? Who will make all of those daily decisions that need to be made in everybody's life?

The law has long recognized the need to provide for the management of your affairs if, for whatever reason, you are unable to make the decisions yourself. You can plan for this situation by legally authorizing another to make your financial and/or medical decisions for you, if you ever become incapable of making them yourself. This transfer of responsibility is most often created by agreement between you and the person you want to assist you, with a legal document known as the power of attorney. If you don't create a power of attorney and you need financial or personal decisions made for you, this is accomplished formally by the courts through the legal tool known as a *guardianship*. This chapter describes both, including the pros and cons of each type of protection.

# GUARDIANSHIPS

A guardianship (sometimes called *conservatorship*) is a court procedure where a relative, friend or other qualified person (called the *guardian*), is appointed by the court to manage the financial and/or personal affairs of another (called the *ward* – the person being cared for). When a guardianship is established, the guardian is given the legal power to "stand in the shoes" of the person being cared for. This means that the guardian makes all of the decisions on behalf and for the benefit of the ward.

### Who Creates a Guardianship?

Guardianships are created by court order, after someone asks through court papers that the guardianship be created. Often, a child or other relative petitions for the guardianship when their parent is no longer capable of handling their own financial and/or personal affairs. If the senior is destitute and without family, the state may bring the court case through the office of the public guardian.

### How Is a Guardianship Created?

Guardianships can *only* be created by court order. The first step is to file a petition in court seeking a judge's permission to establish the guardianship. The petition will: name the person supposedly needing care; identify the person or entity, such as a bank, that the petition requests be named as the service provider; and explain the factual reasons why a guardianship needs to be created. The person supposedly needing care must then be served with court papers informing him or her of the contents of the court papers and the date of the court hearing. A short time later, a hearing is held before a judge, with testimony given under oath, to see whether the facts justify creating the guardianship. This must be established by a very high level of proof.

Otto suffered an emotional collapse, causing him to suffer psychotic delusions. His delusions took the form of a voice commanding him to give all of his money away to strangers on the street. When Otto's children saw their father take a bag of money down Main Street, giving $20 bills to everyone he saw, they knew they had to take action to protect Otto and his estate. Otto was examined by a psychiatrist who diagnosed a psychosis. It was his expert opinion that Otto was incompetent to handle his own affairs. Otto's children filed for a guardianship and Otto's daughter was named as guardian of Otto's estate. She then instructed Otto's bank not to release any more money to Otto and his life savings were preserved to support him in the future.

## What If I Object to the Guardianship?

No guardianship can be created against your wishes without the court listening to your side. This means you have to be served with legal papers seeking to establish the guardianship and that you can fight the proposed guardianship in court. If you do want to fight the case, you should file papers with the court objecting to the proposed guardianship and you should consider hiring an attorney because so much is at stake. Then, you or your attorney can confront the witnesses against you and present evidence on your behalf. The judge can only order the guardianship if the balance of the evidence shows that your welfare would be harmed unless the guardianship is created.

## Are There Different Kinds of Guardianships?

There are two kinds of guardianships: guardianship of the estate and guardianship of the person.

**Guardianship of the Estate.** This is the most common form of guardianship. If you're named the guardian of another's estate, you are given the legal right to control all business and financial affairs. This means, you pay the bills, have the power to sign contracts, collect money owed to the ward, file the tax returns and otherwise control all financial aspects of the ward's estate.

Guardianships of the estate are sometimes created with the consent of the person needing assistance. In such cases, the person needing to be cared for often picks who he or she wants to be guardian and will attend the court hearing to approve the appointment of the guardianship.

**Guardianship of the Person.** A guardianship of the person is a far more drastic step than a guardianship of the estate. It removes the right of the person needing assistance to make personal choices for themselves, such as where to live or what kind of medical care to receive. For this reason, the courts will only allow guardianship of the person if the person needing help is incompetent to make life's decisions. (When a guardianship of the person is created, a guardianship of the estate usually is too.)

---

Oscar suffered a devastating stroke which left him without the power to understand or communicate. The doctors told Oscar's son, Oscar, Jr., that it would be years before Oscar recovered, if ever. Junior decided to apply for a guardianship of the person and the estate of his father so that he could control the management of his father's retail business and could make decisions about his father's medical care and housing needs. The court heard the evidence and granted the request. Thereafter, Oscar Jr. managed his father's entire life, including his business affairs and made the decisions about where his father was to be hospitalized and about the course of his health care.

---

## Are There Safeguards to Protect the Ward?

The law recognizes the potential for abuse and provides protection for wards by supervising and reviewing all actions taken by the guardian to make sure they were appropriate. The court will also require regular financial accounting of the ward's estate. Major decisions may even require the advanced approval of the court. This supervision by the court is a primary difference between a guardianship and a power of attorney. Sadly, however, monitoring of a guardian's activities, in many states, is minimal because of lax judges or inattentive court personnel.

## What Are the Costs of a Guardianship?

A guardianship can be expensive. Under the law, the guardian has the right to be paid for services rendered on behalf of the ward. The court must approve the fees before they are paid. (Family members who serve as their parent's guardian sometimes waive this fee.) If the ward has hired a lawyer for the guardianship estate, the lawyer's fees will also be paid from the estate as approved by the court. There will also be bond fees, since the court usually requires a bond to guarantee good faith and fair dealing in managing the estate. (The ward is a fiduciary to the guardian and therefore legally required to meet the highest standards of ethical conduct and competence in performing his or her duties.)

## Can the Government Bring a Guardianship Action?

Government entities can and do bring guardianship cases to protect older people when there is a demonstrated need to protect the older person's safety or the safety of others. This most frequently occurs in the context of allowing the welfare department to take emergency measures to protect those who are in substantial risk from themselves or to others. Known as an emergency intervention, representatives of a city or county or other government entity can forcibly enter the premises of an aged person and remove them to a hospital or other shelter for their protection. Soon thereafter, hearings will be held to determine whether there was probable cause for the emergency action. If not, the matter will be dropped. If there are legal grounds to proceed, the state can seek involuntary protective services for the endangered adult. If you have any questions about state-initiated guardianships, contact your department of public welfare or the office of adult protective services.

Guardianships can, sometimes, work well to protect those, who through injury, illness or infirmary, are in need of help. This is especially true for those who have a large estate, where the protection of court supervision is important. On the other hand, guardianships can be cumbersome and expensive. For this reason, many seniors prefer to use powers of attorney when they need assistance with their affairs, especially if the person they choose to help them is a child, spouse or other trusted loved one.

## THE POWER OF ATTORNEY

A power of attorney is a legal document that grants someone else, called the "attorney-in-fact," the authority to act on your behalf. The power granted can be broad or limited, both in terms of what can be managed and the time during which the power of attorney remains in full force and effect.

When you sign a power of attorney, you have the right to establish the rules. You may wish to grant the attorney complete control over your financial life, or you may restrict the right to act on your behalf to a single task; for example, selling your house. You can also limit the time during which the power of attorney is valid. In other words, a power of attorney is only as broad or narrow as you define it in the document creating the power of attorney.

When you sign a power of attorney, you give another person the power to manage your affairs, according to the terms set forth in the document itself. You do not give up ownership of the property, nor does the title of your property pass to anyone else.

Your power of attorney ends whenever you say it will in the document. It can also end upon your death or, unless otherwise provided (see discussion of "The Durable Power of Attorney"), in the event of your incapacity. You can also revoke a power of attorney in writing at any time (see below).

Your attorney-in-fact is in a fiduciary relationship with you and owes you the highest standard of performance. Thus, your attorney-in-fact cannot commingle your money with his or her own funds, nor can your attorney take any action that would amount to a conflict of interest. If he or she does not meet these fiduciary obligations to you, you can sue for damages. However, in order to sue, you have to know there's been misconduct. Since there is no court oversight of the work of your attorney-in-fact, that may not be easy. Thus, it is important that you only delegate this powerful mandate to someone you explicitly trust.

There are two different types of power of attorney: the simple power of attorney and the durable power of attorney.

## The Simple Power of Attorney

The simple power of attorney is the basic model. It allows you to delegate the power to manage part or all of your affairs, even though you are competent to handle the matter yourself. For example, if you are going to take a world cruise and will be away from home for six months, you might sign a power of attorney allowing your son to pay your bills, collect rent from your tenant and otherwise manage your business affairs. Under the law, a simple power of attorney terminates upon your incapacity.

## The Durable Power of Attorney

The principle difference between a simple power of attorney and a durable power of attorney is that a durable power of attorney continues to be effective during your incapacity. In fact, that is the whole point of a durable power of attorney.

A durable power of attorney can go into effect immediately upon signing. In this situation, the power of attorney is a simple one while you are competent but continues if you become incapacitated. You can also sign a power of attorney that does not go into effect until and unless you are incapacitated. This is sometimes called a "springing power of attorney."

Durable and springing powers of attorney can eliminate the need for a guardianship if you become incapacitated. A

durable power of attorney for health care can also delegate
your health-care decisions (see Chapter 7). A durable power
of attorney ceases to exist upon your death. You can revoke
it at any time, so long as the revocation occurs while you
are competent to make the decision.

You can create a power of attorney by signing the form
in front of a notary public. You can also record the power of
attorney at your County Recorder's office but that is not
necessary for the power of attorney to be effective. You can
obtain a power of attorney form at most stationery stores
with the legal phrasing required in your state, or, if you
prefer, a lawyer can prepare a power of attorney for a very
modest fee – typically $50 or less.

In order to revoke a power of attorney, you should sign a
document called a Notice of Revocation. This document
must also be signed in front of a notary. You can then
record the revocation with the County Recorder, although
it's not a legal requirement. Once you have revoked the
power of attorney, be sure to deliver a copy to the person you
named as your attorney-in-fact and to any businesses or
financial institutions where your attorney-in-fact has done
business on your behalf. (Otherwise, they may continue to
engage in business with your former attorney-in-fact. In
such a case, you could be held financially responsible.)

---

Oscar signed a durable power of attorney, naming his son Junior to
manage his retail business if he were to become incapacitated. Two days
later, Oscar was hit by a car and went into a coma. Junior took over
operation of the business during his father's incapacity. When Oscar
became well again, he regained control of his business because he was no
longer incapacitated.

Otto didn't get around to preparing a power of attorney. He was hit
by the same car as his brother Oscar and also went into a coma. Otto's
daughter, Ora, tried to run his business, but soon discovered that the
bank and Otto's business vendors would not deal with her because she had
no legal authority to act on her father's behalf. She had to file for a
guardianship in order to get the power to keep the business running until
her father was well again.

---

As you can see, powers of attorney can make life easier
for you and your family. Durable powers of attorney can be

especially valuable if you are ever incapacitated. Moreover, they are easy to prepare, they are effective and they are generally safe – so long as the person you name as attorney-in-fact is trustworthy.

# 15

# NURSING HOMES & LONG-TERM CARE

Mention the phrase, "long-term care" to someone and you just might hear an involuntary shudder. Why? Many view the term as a tactful way of saying, "locked away in a nursing home." Nursing homes, in turn, bring to mind horror stories about morbid and filthy conditions, where old people are sent away to die amidst the smell of urine and the neglect of the nursing home staff.

The truth about nursing homes and other long-term care options available to you and your family are much more positive. While it's true that some long-term care facilities are filthy and neglectful, the majority of nursing homes are clean, well-run custodial care facilities that provide a high quality of service. Moreover, nursing home residents possess enforceable legal rights that protect them against abuse and neglect.

Before describing nursing homes and your rights as a patient, the next section describes alternatives or transition care when full nursing care may not be needed, but some care is.

# ALTERNATIVES TO NURSING HOMES

Many people find they can avoid placement in a nursing home by making use of community services designed to *prevent* the need for nursing home placement. Here are some other options to consider:

## Staying at Home

Sometimes seniors end up in a nursing facility because they cannot live in complete independence but do not know about available in-home services which could allow them to remain in their home. Community programs such as Meals on Wheels bring hot, nutritious meals to your door. Volunteer programs, like Senior Companion, give lonely senior citizens some friendship and help with things like writing letters and running errands. Homemaking assistance may be charged on an income-basis sliding scale, and home health care can be paid for by Medicare when medically necessary. Many seniors are able to maintain their independence by taking advantage of these services. Contact your Area Agency on Aging or local senior center for more details.

## Living With a Child or Relative

Many families would like to take their older loved ones into their homes but do not believe it's practical. This is not always true. In addition to the services mentioned above, many communities have respite care facilities which will take seniors for a short time to allow the family to take a vacation or have some privacy. Senior day care is a growing industry. Community multi-purpose senior centers provide excellent services for seniors and their families through recreational opportunities, by providing low-cost meals and as a clearing house for the wealth of information available to help seniors and their families.

## Residential Care Facilities

Some seniors need assistance, but not so much that they require a nursing home. A licensed residential care facility may be just the ticket. Residential care facilities allow seniors to live in a structured and sheltered environment for less money than a nursing home, because nursing care is not provided. Residential homes offer assistance with medication, meals, homemaker services and security. Residential care facilities usually have minimum physical requirements, and can force you to leave if your condition falls below the established minimum. Be sure and ask about minimum health requirements before you decide to move into a residential care facility.

If you have any further questions about nursing homes, residential care facilities or community services available for the benefit of seniors or their families, contact your local Area Agency on Aging, a local chapter of the American Association of Retired People (AARP) or a private geriatric care manager or community social worker.

# NURSING HOME CARE

Nursing homes are medical facilities that provide long-term care to their patients. There are approximately 19,000 nursing homes in operation in the country, housing over 1.5 million residents. The majority of nursing homes are for-profit enterprises. Nursing homes are licensed and supervised by the state. Federal nursing home reform laws include extensive resident rights and mandates for all nursing homes, including comprehensive assessment and care based on that assessment.

If you or a loved one face the prospect of placement in a nursing home, you need to understand the nature of the services provided in these long-term care facilities and your rights under the law to ensure that you receive high quality care. The rest of this chapter discusses your options and how to pay for them, as well as your legal rights.

## Nursing Homes Provide Four Basic Services

**Personal Care.** Most of the services provided by a nursing home are custodial. That is, residents are provided assistance with the basic tasks of life: eating, hygiene, dressing, etc.

**Nursing Care.** Licensed Practical Nurses and Registered Nurses are on staff at nursing homes to provide basic nursing care as ordered by a doctor, such as administering injections and catheterizations, and monitoring blood pressure and body temperature.

**Medical Care.** A nursing home is not a hospital where serious illnesses are treated. However, medical treatment for less serious maladies are often rendered in the nursing home, usually provided by the resident's personal physician.

**Residential Care.** A nursing home is also a place where people live. The level and quality of nursing home residential services will vary, but includes room, board, organized recreational activities, security and social programs.

## RESIDENT RIGHTS

Nursing home patients have legal rights guaranteed by the laws in most states. Usually, these rights will include the following:

- Free choice of attending physician and the right to participate in care planning
- Freedom from physical or mental abuse
- Freedom from chemical or physical restraints applied for the benefit of the staff and not the protection of the patient
- Privacy and confidentiality of medical and personal records

- The right to organize and join residents' or family groups
- The right to the services of a State Ombudsman
- The right to express grievances without suffering retaliation or discrimination
- The right to participate in social, religious and community activities
- The right to see the results of any state or federal inspection of the facility
- The right to receive a written cost disclosure notice before entering the facility
- An environment that is clean, sanitary and in good repair
- A diet consisting of a variety of good-quality foods
- The right to dignity and respect in personal care
- An opportunity for the patient to purchase drugs and medical supplies from a pharmacy or other source of choice

Knowing you have rights and enforcing them are two different things. Many people involved with nursing home care aren't aware of the enforcement mechanisms available to them. More often, there is the very real and understandable fear of angering the people you depend on for your, or your loved one's, care.

However, enforcing your legal rights should not be feared. Great progress has been made in this field. Today, residents and their families have real clout to ensure high quality of nursing home care.

In fact, dispute resolution is a normal part of the give and take of nursing home living. Staff retaliation against residents who speak up for their rights is becoming a behavior of the past.

Unless you exercise your legal rights, they are nothing more than abstract concepts written on paper. That means, you have to be ready to be courteously assertive in enforcing your rights to respectful service and quality care. Here's how:

## Talk With the Person Involved

If you're having problems with the care you or your loved one is receiving, it's usually best to try and solve them in an informal and business-like way. Ask the offending care giver to have a private chat. In a noncondemning way, explain why you're unhappy and back-up your claim with as many specific examples as possible. Then, listen to their side of the story. If both parties are reasonable, most disputes can be settled in a friendly and constructive manner.

## Bring in the Administration

Your nursing home must have a formal program of dispute resolution in place to deal with conflicts. If you cannot solve your problems privately, you should exercise your right to seek redress of your grievances through the dispute resolution procedure established by the nursing home. This is usually not a mere shell of a right without real substance. Most administrators realize that residents and family are the source of the nursing home's future business and many are sensitive to resident and family complaints. Moreover, administrators know that your continued unhappiness can lead to state involvement in the dispute.

## Contact the State Ombudsman

If you cannot achieve satisfaction within the nursing home itself, it is time to call in your State Ombudsman. Thanks to the efforts of nursing home resident advocates, each state now has an office of Long-Term Care Ombudsman, whose job it is to investigate and resolve complaints made by, or on behalf of, residents. Ombudsmen are well-trained, understand and care about resident rights and are generally committed to solving the disputes that arise under their jurisdiction. The nursing home legally must provide you with the address and telephone number of the Ombudsman office.

## Report the Home to State Authorities

If the Ombudsman can't help you or if the problem is serious, such as neglect or physical abuse, report the home to the state licensing agency or Department of Health, or the Medicaid Fraud Control Unit if the home receives Medicaid funds. That should get the attention of the administration, since the state has the legal right to close the nursing home if the environment is unsanitary or residents are abused or neglected. In such serious cases, you're doing your loved one and the other residents in the home a favor by bringing the force of law to the problem.

## File a Lawsuit Against the Nursing Home

If you or a loved one is injured or neglected by the nursing home, or if the administration has threatened to infringe upon your legal rights, it might be worth contacting a lawyer to see whether the facility can be sued for damages and/or forced by court order to respect your rights under the law.

# PAYING FOR NURSING HOME CARE

As you will recall from Chapter 2, Medicare does not pay for custodial care in a nursing home. Unless you are rich, paying for nursing home care will be a major family concern and financial burden. There are three primary ways to pay for nursing home care:

## Medicaid

Medicaid pays for nursing home care. However, you have to become impoverished in order to qualify for the program or take legal steps to preserve family assets by preplanning for Medicaid eligibility. Also, every nursing home does not accept Medicaid patients. Please refer to Chapter 5 for more details.

## Paying Out of Your Own Funds

Unless you qualify for Medicaid, you will have to pay for your nursing home care out of your own pocket. Since nursing home care is quite expensive, ranging generally between $2,000 and $3,000 a month, depending on where you live, many families share the cost among members so that their parent or parents can receive the best care possible. It is also important to note that the monthly charge you will pay as a private resident will be far higher than the fee that will be paid for the same care by Medicaid. Thus, while it's not supposed to happen, in the "real world" you may find that you can't get admission into the better nursing homes unless the administration believes your care will be privately paid for a period of time, before you go on Medicaid.

## Buy Nursing Home Insurance

There is a relatively new insurance policy being sold today, known as nursing home insurance or long-term care insurance. The purpose of these policies is to defray the cost of long-term care so as to preserve family assets.

Long-term care insurance is a topic you should definitely think about when planning for your retirement years. But the real question is; is the insurance worth the price? That depends, of course, on your individual circumstances. If you have a large estate and can afford the expensive premiums, the insurance you receive may provide significant protection of your assets. However, if you can't really afford the premiums or if nursing home care will deplete your estate regardless of the benefits of insurance, you should probably plan instead for Medicaid eligibility. It is also important to note that some consumer groups, like Consumers Union, are not fans of long-term care insurance nor are many writers in the field of senior citizen affairs.

If you are thinking of purchasing such insurance to protect yourself against the costs of future nursing home placement, be sure to ask many questions before you sign on the dotted line. For example:

**How High Are the Benefits?** Nursing homes can cost in the thousands of dollars per month. If your insurance would only pay a few hundred dollars a month in benefits, the protection you receive may not be worth the cost of the premiums.

**Are Preexisting Conditions Excluded?** Before you buy the policy, if you have a condition that requires nursing home care, the preexisting condition could be used by the insurance company to get out of paying for your nursing home care.

**Is There an Alzheimer's Disease Exclusion?** Alzheimer's disease is a merciless destroyer that can strike any family. Ultimately, nearly all Alzheimer's disease victims must be placed in a nursing home. If your insurance will not pay benefits for Alzheimer's disease related nursing home care, it is probably not worth buying.

**Must You Be Hospitalized Before Being Admitted to a Nursing Home for Benefits to Be Paid?** According to Consumer's Union, 60 percent of all nursing home placements are made *without* prior hospitalization, thus such a clause may make the policy of little value.

**What Are the Time Limits of Coverage?** Many nursing home residents live for years after their admission. If the length of coverage is short, the policy may be inadequate to protect family assets.

**Is There a Long Waiting Period?** If you must be in the nursing facility for a long time before benefits are paid, the cost of nursing home care may impoverish you before your insurance benefits kick in. In such circumstances, what good is buying insurance?

**Is the Policy Renewable?** If the policy can be canceled based on your health, it does not provide much protection.

## INVOLUNTARY DISCHARGES

One of the most serious problems facing nursing home residents is the threat of involuntary discharge. For many of the elderly, being forced to leave a nursing home is like being forced out of their own home. A nursing facility quickly becomes home for the residents who live there. That's where security is. That's where friends are. That's where life is predictable and comfortable. Being forced to leave against one's will can be a truly traumatic event.

The law has come to recognize that unscrupulous nursing homes might try to get rid of patients who go on Medicaid or who assert their rights, and has created resident legal rights to prevent unfair and unwarranted involuntary discharge. Here's an overview:

### Discharge By the Nursing Home

Federal and state law restricts the ability of a nursing home to discharge you against your will. In particular, you cannot be discharged or threatened with discharge because you have complained about the level of care or because you have sought to enforce your rights. In other words, retaliatory discharge is not permitted.

As with most laws, there are exceptions to the law's prohibition:

- You can be discharged for medical reasons, such as needing to be in a hospital for an extended period of time.
- You can be discharged for failing to pay your bill.

- You can be discharged to protect your own welfare or that of other residents.
- You can be discharged if the nursing home loses its Medicare or Medicaid certification, if that is how you are paying for your care.

You have important procedural rights if your nursing home tries to force you to leave. For example, you have the right to be *notified* ahead of the discharge date of the action that the nursing home plans to take. Normally, the minimum advance notice is 30 days. You also have the right to appeal, if you receive such a notice. Your method of appeal will be different in each state. Ask your nursing home administrator, the Ombudsman's office or your Area Agency on Aging for details.

---

Otto was in a nursing home and didn't like the food. He complained to the nurse and was told to, "Shut up and eat." He then complained to the administrator. The administrator apologized for the rudeness of the staff but stated that the food was good and nutritious and met all requirements of the state laws. Otto then called in the State Ombudsman, who was unable to make him happy. About this time, the staff got tired of worrying about Otto's food likes and dislikes and the hospital served a written notice on Otto giving him 30 days to leave the facility. But Otto knew his legal rights and resisted the discharge. He won his appeal and was permitted to remain in the nursing home because he was able to show that the only reason the hospital wanted him out was because they resented his complaints about the food – an insufficient cause for discharge under the law.

Oscar also lived in a nursing home. He too complained about his food, but he did more than that. When unhappy with his meals, he would throw food, the plate and the silverware at the staff and other residents. Things got worse when he began to play his television late at night and refused to keep the sound low. When people asked him to turn the set down, he threatened to stick a fork in their mouths. And he repeatedly hit other residents with his fist. The nursing home sought to have Oscar discharged and won when Oscar appealed based on the physical threat Oscar's behavior posed to the staff and other residents.

## The Utilization Review Board

If Medicare or Medicaid is paying your nursing home cost, you are only eligible for continuing benefits if the care being given is medically necessary, if the home you are in offers the requisite level of care and if a periodic review is made to determine your continued need to remain in the nursing facility on benefits. This is called the utilization review, and it is conducted by a review board made up of professionals who work at your nursing care facility. If the board finds that you no longer require the care, you can be forced to leave the home against your will or be forced to pay for the cost of care out of your own pocket.

If you are advised that your benefits are going to be cut based on the utilization review, you have the same appeal rights you would have if you disagreed with any other Medicaid or Medicare determination.

## The Temporary Leave

If you leave the nursing home for a short time, for example to visit your family or because you had to be hospitalized, your nursing home can discharge you under certain conditions.

All states are required to have a bed-hold policy. Many states guarantee that you cannot be discharged from the nursing home if you are absent for a short time. (The time is typically five to seven days.) After you've been absent from the home longer than your guaranteed time, your nursing home can discharge you and give your bed to someone else. If you're on Medicaid and discharged, you have the right to the next available bed at your former nursing home. If you leave the nursing home, they must give you a written notice stating your rights under state law to keep your place in the nursing home during a temporary absence.

# 16

# DEATH & FUNERAL ARRANGEMENTS

Death comes to all of us, hopefully later rather than sooner, but it always comes. Death is emotional and expensive. Funerals can cost thousands or even tens of thousands of dollars. As seniors grow older, death becomes an increasingly familiar companion, as beloved peers pass away and the reality of personal mortality becomes less abstract and more clearly focused.

Death also involves legal rights of the deceased and the family. Knowing these rights may not alleviate the pain of loss, but it can allow this difficult time to be lived with more dignity and more healing, and be more conducive to a smooth transition from grief into the carrying on of life.

When a loved one dies, there are many arrangements that must be made. The body's disposition. The notification of family and friends. The funeral arrangements. Sometimes, with all of the coming and going, people can be pressured into making decisions that are expensive and which may not have been made were it not for the emotion and confusion of the moment.

## KNOWING YOUR RIGHTS

The best way to avoid such troubles is to know your rights before time of need. Here are the answers to some commonly asked questions about death and the law:

### Can I Determine the Disposition of My Body?

Generally, no. With the possible exception of organ or body donations to science, your expressed wishes about disposition are not legally binding, even if the expression is contained in your will. Your best assurance of having your wishes followed is to discuss the matter ahead of time with your family or the person who will be in charge of your final disposition, so there's no mistake or confusion. Making arrangements ahead of time will also go a long way toward making sure your desires are followed.

### Does My Body Have to Be Embalmed?

No. The purpose of embalming is to preserve the body. Many people believe that embalming is required by state law, but it isn't true. Some mortuaries push for embalming because it is a money-maker, or because of the fact that a body not embalmed will probably have to have a closed casket at the funeral due to health and aesthetic reasons.

### Does There Have to Be an Autopsy?

That depends. An autopsy need only be conducted if the person died without an attending physician or if the death occurred under questionable circumstances.

### Can I Be Stopped From Donating My Body or Organs?

Probably not. The laws in all fifty states and the District of Columbia allow you to bequeath any part or all of your body for medical, educational, research, therapy or transplantation. Many state laws allow your choice about such matters to be binding and enforceable by law, or at least allow for the removal of your organs without permission of your family, if you have legally filled out an organ donor card. (You may be familiar with organ donation cards that can be filled out in connection with renewing your license to drive.)

### Can I Preplan My Own Funeral?

Absolutely. However, there are some things you should know before you do:

**Paying for Your Funeral in Advance.** You can preplan your funeral with a mortuary and/or cemetery. Before you actually die, you can pick out the type of coffin you want, the extent of mortuary services, such as whether you want embalming, the style of plaque and the location where you want to be buried. However, with the exception of buying your burial plot, it may not be wise to pay for everything ahead of time. There are scam artists out there who pray on the elderly and their desire to arrange their funerals ahead of time. Also, under some pre-paid funeral plans you must make monthly payments toward your funeral until you die. Thus, if you live a long time, you could end up over-paying for your funeral.

Rather than paying for your funeral in advance, think about using life insurance or a specially designated interest-bearing account to pay for the services at the time of death. Many financial institutions will allow you to establish an account earmarked for this specific purpose. Ask your banker for more details.

**Joining a Cremation Society.** There are cremation societies you can join and pay ahead of time for services. For a one-time-only modest fee, you can become a "member." Then, when you die, all that is required is notice to the society and they will pick up the body and handle the cremation according to your instructions. This procedure is sometimes called direct cremation. (There are also direct burials that can save you and your family money, if you don't want a funeral.)

**Joining a Memorial Society.** Memorial societies are nonprofit organizations that offer information about funerals and arrange with local funeral directors to provide services to members at reduced cost. You must pay a small fee to join a memorial society. However, most societies do not require you to pay for services in advance.

### What Are the Rules of Cremation?

Cremation is growing in popularity in the United States. Some people choose cremation because of its economy. Others have a philosophical belief that cremation is the best method of body disposition.

Cremation is legal everywhere in the United States, although the rules which govern the practice vary from location to location. Many people have questions about the legal ins and outs of cremation, including:

**Does There Have to Be a Casket?** In most states, all that is required is a suitable container. (Some states go so far as to legally forbid funeral homes or cremation services to require coffins.) A suitable container is usually one that protects the health of crematory workers, that covers the body and is of combustible material.

**What Happens to the Remains After Cremation?** The remains can be buried in a cemetery, interred in a mausoleum, returned to the family in a cremation urn, or scattered at sea or in some other legally authorized place and manner.

**How Do I Know the Ashes Are Those of My Loved One?** The law is very specific about this. Crematoriums are under strict guidelines concerning the identification of remains and the ashes after cremation. Criminal and/or civil sanctions can be (and have been) imposed for failing to properly identify the remains being cremated or for failing to segregate ashes.

## How Can I Be Assured of Grave Maintenance?

Most states require cemeteries to create a trust fund, usually called an endowment care fund, which is used to guarantee that the cemetery and your grave will be properly maintained. Some cemeteries include the cost of perpetual care in their charge for the plot or crypt. Others add a surcharge which is placed in the trust fund. Such trust funds are often administered by a state agency.

## Can I Be Buried In a National Cemetery?

If you served honorably in the Armed Forces, whether in war or peace, the answer is yes. As a veteran with an honorable discharge, you have the right to free burial in a National Cemetery, a headstone and a U.S. flag for your family. (This does not mean you can choose any cemetery. Space is growing tight and some national cemeteries, most notably, Arlington National Cemetery, have had to put restrictions in place.)

Otto wanted to be cremated. In his will, he directed the executor of his will to see to it that his wishes were granted. Otto's son, Junior, was a member of a religion that viewed cremation as morally wrong. After Otto's death, Junior prevented the cremation from taking place and had his father buried instead. The executor could do nothing to stop it.

Oscar was a veteran. He wanted to be buried in a National Cemetery. The nearest such cemetery was in his city, but that cemetery was full. The next nearest available National Cemetery was 250 miles away. Oscar's family decided to bury him in a local cemetery instead and pay for the burial themselves.

Otto and Oscar's next door neighbor Eddie legally signed a body donor card leaving his entire body to the local medical school for scientific purposes. Eddie had died of Alzheimer's disease, a little understood malady of the brain, and so the school was very pleased to have the donation. Eddie's daughter was opposed to body donations, and she tried to prevent the school from taking possession of Eddie's body. Because her state enforced donor card bequests of body parts, she was unable to prevail.

# PLANNING A FUNERAL

The American way of death has been studied, written about and explored in film and television. Still, many of us choose to remain ignorant about such matters until the time of need arrives. After all, who wants to dwell on depressing information?

Still, the realities must be dealt with. Here are some of the issues you will be dealing with should you plan a funeral, whether your own or that of a loved one:

## Mortuary Services

Mortuary services include picking the remains up from the place of death, embalming or holding the body in cold storage until the funeral, securing signatures and death certificates, body preparation if there is to be a viewing, and use of mortuary facilities for viewing or storage purposes.

## Finding the Final Resting Place

If a burial is going to be planned, a plot must be purchased. That means you are going to have to take a tour of the cemetery and find the spot you want. (The brighter and more picturesque, the more expensive the plot.) "Family plots" can also be obtained so that family members can be buried in the same place. If a mausoleum is desired, the space therein for the internment must be chosen and bought. You can, of course, prepurchase your plot. But be aware that once purchased, the cemetery will not buy the land back. In all likelihood, you will also have to purchase a funeral vault, a concrete, metal or wood lining in which the coffin is placed. The purpose of a vault is to keep the grave from sinking in. Vaults are not usually required by state law, although many municipalities do have laws mandating them. Most cemeteries require vaults. However, if you can find a cemetery that does not force you to buy a vault, you can save money on the cost of the burial.

## Funeral Arrangements

There's a lot more to planning a funeral than you may at first believe. For example, if the deceased is going to be buried, a casket must be chosen. Also, the plaque or headstone, if one is desired. You have to plan the service if there is to be one, select the eulogizers and clergy, purchase flowers, if that is your desire, and invite friends and family you wish to attend, all this within days of the death.

With all of this to do, plus meet the emotional needs of the family, it's not surprising that many people come away from the situation believing they've paid more than they should have, that the services were poorly provided, or some other complaint. If you're unhappy with the funeral services you received, you can obtain consumer arbitration through the Funeral Service Consumer Assistance Program. The program has many benefits to consumers:

- Binding arbitration is available, allowing for quick and inexpensive final resolution of the dispute.

- The program is available to anyone who has complaints about a funeral home's services during the previous 12 months – that means you can get over the worst of your grief before filing and not forfeit your rights due to passage of time.
- The arbitration relies on written testimony and thus you will not have to travel or take time off from work.
- The arbitration is free.
- If you win and your funeral director refuses to abide by the decision, there is a Consumer Security Fund that will pay the restitution you are owed.

For more information about the program, contact your local funeral director, or write: the Funeral Service Consumer Assistance Program, 2250 E. Devon Ave., Ste. 250, Des Plaines, IL 60018. They also have a toll free number: (800) 662-7666.

For more information about the rules governing funerals and funeral directors, contact: The Federal Trade Commission, Sixth and Pennsylvania Ave., N.W. Washington, D.C. 20036.

# 17

# AGE
# DISCRIMINATION

Many seniors face a difficult and disturbing problem. It is prejudice. Talk with most people over 50 and you will be told that prejudice and discrimination based on age is very real in this country. Some of this prejudice is subtle and some is overtly expressed. In whatever way it is expressed, the consequences of age-based prejudice can be devastating to your self esteem and personal finances, and can even adversely affect your health.

This chapter introduces you to your legal rights to prevent discrimination. Most of the text deals with federal law. Your state may also have laws to protect you against this unwarranted form of abuse.

## DISCRIMINATION IN EMPLOYMENT

There are a lot of myths concerning our older years that cause some employers to engage in unwarranted job discrimination. For example, some employers mistakenly believe that older workers miss substantially more time from work due to illness and will not hire a qualified applicant merely because they are considered old. Other employers, thinking about their own bottom line, let older and higher-paid workers go so they can hire younger workers who may be willing to work for less money. Some older workers are also discriminated against when they are not trained as well as their younger counterparts, thereby reducing their chances for promotion and wage increase.

Federal Law prohibits such age discrimination in employment in a law called the *Age Discrimination in Employment Act* (ADEA). Here are some of the ADEAs important protections:

- It protects people over 40 from all forms of age discrimination in hiring, promotion and the terms and conditions of employment.
- The protection provided by the law is broad. It covers working employees, job applicants, labor unions, employment agencies, and government entities.

There is another statute that protects you against discrimination in worker benefits. It's called the Older Workers Benefit Protection Act. This law prevents your employer from giving you a different level of health insurance and different and better benefits to younger workers.

## FEDERAL REMEDIES

If you believe you have been the victim of age discrimination, here are some steps you can take:

### File a Charge With EEOC

The Equal Employment Opportunity Commission (EEOC) is the federal agency that deals with cases of discrimination over a wide variety of fronts, ranging from racial discrimination to sexual harassment to age discrimination. If you believe you have suffered an act of discrimination, your complaint must be filed within 180 days of the discriminatory act. *This is a strict deadline*, so don't delay taking action.

The charge should provide the following information:

- Your name, address and telephone number.
- The name, address and telephone number of the discriminating party.
- The nature of the discrimination (for example, being refused a promotion or denied worker benefits).
- The facts that form the basis of the charge. For example, if your boss trained younger people on the company's new computer system – training necessary to be eligible for promotion – but refused to give you the training even though you were otherwise qualified to receive it, you could contact the EEOC and file a complaint. (If you file a complaint, be as specific as possible. Try to answer the questions: Who did what? When did they do it? Where was it done? Who else witnessed the discrimination?)
- The reasons the discriminating party gave for their actions.
- The reasons you believe the actions taken by the discriminating party were wrong.
- If you can, supply the EEOC with copies of employee policy manuals, copies of your employment file and any other document you believe relevant to the charges you are making.

You can file the charge in the mail or on the telephone, but those who work in the field will tell you that your best bet is to complain in person at one of the EEOC field offices. For the EEOC office nearest you, look in your telephone book, or call the Washington, D.C., headquarters at (202) 663-4264.

## YOUR CLAIM CAN BE KEPT CONFIDENTIAL

If you do not want to be identified to your employer as having filed a charge, you can take steps to see that your wishes are respected:

## File a "Complaint" Rather Than a "Charge"

Your complaint can indicate that you do not want your identity revealed. In such a case, your identity will be kept confidential, absent your written authority to reveal your name, or a court order.

## Tip Off the EEOC

The EEOC has the power to investigate cases of discrimination even if no formal charge or complaint has been filed by an individual. Thus, you may be able to spark an investigation by contacting the EEOC as a whistleblower, rather than as a formal complainant.

The EEOC usually tries to problem solve before they resort to litigation. Thus, if you file a complaint, expect the agency to seek conciliation before resorting to a case in court.

If you go through the EEOC conciliation process and the matter is not solved, you can bring an independent action. Be aware that there is a time limit. You must file suit within 60 days of charging age discrimination with the EEOC. You will also want to consult a lawyer.

In the cases where EEOC files suit, you are usually precluded from doing so in your own name, unless you have filed an action before the EEOC's action. The EEOC action also supersedes litigation by state agencies.

## STATE ADMINISTRATIVE REMEDIES

Age discrimination is also illegal under most state laws, and most states have enforcement agencies to prevent and punish it. If you file a claim with the state, the matter will usually be handled out-of-court through administrative hearings. Going this route, rather than suing, can save you money, since you don't have to pay a lawyer or finance the lawsuit.

## File a Lawsuit

You can bring an action in court to enforce your rights under the ADEA. If you choose to do so, it's a good idea to retain an attorney who understands the law and procedure involved in bringing such cases to court.

## Remedies Available to You Under the ADEA

If you sue, the ADEA provides the remedies the court can award you. The purpose of legal action under the ADEA is to restore you to the economic position you would have occupied were it not for the discrimination. This can include an order for back pay, an order forcing the discriminating company to hire you if you were not given a job due to discrimination, an order compelling a promotion and the reinstatement of fringe benefits. The ADEA also permits double damages in cases of willful discrimination. However, unlike some state laws, you are not permitted to be awarded damages because of pain and suffering.

> Otto worked as a salesman. His sales record was the best in his firm and his past employment history proved that he was a capable manager. When a sales supervisor position became available, Otto tried to get the job. However, the position was given to a thirty-year-old who had no management experience. When Otto asked his boss why he wasn't given the job, the boss replied, "Because I believe in promoting young people. They stay on the job longer." Otto brought suit and was awarded the money he would have earned had he been given the promotion. The court also compelled Otto's employer to make him a sales supervisor.

## File a Lawsuit Under State Laws

You can file a lawsuit based on the laws of your state rather than federal law. You may decide to take this action if your state permits damages for pain and suffering, rather than, or in addition to, seeking federal government assistance.

> Oscar was fired so that two younger people could be hired to take his place. Oscar had worked for the same company for 25 years and was hit hard by the company's lack of loyalty. Oscar fell into despondency as a result of his firing and he attempted suicide. He was hospitalized for depression and treated. His medical bills were $25,000. When he hired an attorney to assist him, he was advised to sue in state court under state anti-discrimination laws, rather than under the ADEA so that he could seek damages for his pain and suffering.

This concludes our discussion of employment discrimination. If you believe you have suffered from illegal conduct by an employer, potential employer or labor union, consult with a senior advocacy group, a law school legal clinic, legal aid or an attorney so you can obtain a complete understanding on the quality of your case and the remedies available to you. Many attorneys who bring cases against employers who discriminate will give you a free initial consultation, although you should ask about that issue before you make an appointment.

## OTHER FORMS OF AGE DISCRIMINATION

Discrimination in employment isn't the only form of discrimination seniors confront.

### Discrimination in Medical Care

A less obvious form of discrimination that sometimes is directed at older people takes place in health care. The discrimination goes something like this: you go into your doctor's complaining of a malady. Your doctor performs a cursory exam, shrugs and says, "It's just old age."

Sometimes this lackadaisical attitude causes no harm, but at other times, it can prevent you from receiving the same vigorous medical care you would receive if you were twenty years younger. This can lead to tragedy. Serious illnesses may go undiagnosed or years from your life can be lost because of inadequate care.

You can combat this form of prejudice by understanding your rights as a patient. (See the discussion on informed consent and informed refusal in Chapter 7.) If you do not believe a doctor is being sufficiently aggressive, get a second opinion. Also, make sure your doctor is knowledgeable in the care and treatment of older people and enjoys treating them. If yours doesn't, contact your local medical society and ask for a doctor who practices in the field of geriatrics. Also, ask your older friends for the names of their doctors if they are pleased with the treatment they receive.

## Discrimination in Transportation

Transportation discrimination can come in many forms. It may be the insurance company that refuses you reasonably-priced auto insurance, or which arbitrarily raises premiums, using a minor accident or claim as an excuse. It may be the public transportation system that is not accessible to the disabled.

There are laws that seek to prevent older people from being treated differently because of their age or physical ability. For example, the *Americans with Disabilities Act* calls for public transportation to be accessible to the disabled. The 1973 Rehabilitation Act protects people with restricted mobility from discrimination in any program or activity which is federally funded. Many states have laws prohibiting age discrimination in auto insurance.

## Discrimination in Credit

Some older people, particularly women, believe they are discriminated against in matters of credit. Such age discrimination is against the law. The *Equal Credit Opportunity Act* (ECOA) says it's illegal to discriminate against you when you apply for credit because of your age or because you are widowed. (It also protects against other forms of credit discrimination, such as discrimination based on race or gender.) The law protects you when dealing with any creditor who regularly extends credit, such as banks, department stores, credit card companies and the like.

Here are some of the credit protections you have under the law:

- You cannot be discouraged from applying because of your age or marital status.
- You cannot be asked whether you are widowed or divorced, if you are applying for an unsecured loan in your own name. (This right may not apply in community property states.)
- A creditor cannot take your age into account when determining whether to grant credit, except under limited conditions. (For example, a creditor can take age into account to see if your income might be reduced because you are about to retire.)

If you suspect that you have been discriminated against, here is what to do:

- Complain to the prospective creditor and let them know they may have violated the law.
- Check with your state Attorney General's office to see if any state laws against credit discrimination have been violated.
- Report violations to the Federal Trade Commission at Sixth Street and Pennsylvania Ave., N.W., Washington, D.C. 20580, (202) 326-2000.
- Bring an action in Federal Court. If you are successful, you can recover any actual damages and be awarded a penalty, and receive compensation for attorneys' fees. However, the amount of damages in such cases may be limited, so be sure the "benefit" you could receive if you win the case is worth the "burden" in costs and time of bringing the case to court.

Discrimination based on age is a social wrong that America is finally beginning to recognize as a serious problem. But prevention depends on you. Only by knowing your rights and by being assertive in protecting them can you prevent yourself and others from suffering the effects of age prejudice. For more information on what you can do to protect yourself, contact the following sources:

- Your local Area Agency on Aging
- Your local chapter of the AARP
- The National Senior Citizens' Law Center in Washington, D.C. (see Appendix 8)
- A local attorney who practices in the field of elder law
- A local chapter of the senior advocacy organization, The Gray Panthers.

# CONCLUSION

There is an old adage that says knowledge is power. But that wisdom does not go far enough. Knowledge is only the potential for power. The wisdom that comes from knowledge only becomes power when it is acted upon. Until then, it is like some inert substance waiting for a catalyst to bring it into full potential.

Helping you access both aspects of power, the knowledge and the implementation, have been the point of this book. Whether in the area of Medicare, nursing homes, retirement or preventing discrimination, this book's purpose has been to inform you of the legal principles you need to understand as an involved senior and to give you the tools you need to take that knowledge and translate it into conscious action. In that way, you will be at the cause of the events of your life and not at the effect. That is true power. And when you get right down to it, isn't that what living life – as opposed to passively experiencing it – is all about?

# APPENDICES

# APPENDIX 1 – SUMMARY OF MEDICARE PART A BENEFITS, 1993

(Source: *The 1993 Guide to Health Insurance for People With Medicare*)

| Services | Benefit | Medicare Pays | You Pay |
|---|---|---|---|
| HOSPITALIZATION<br>Semiprivate room and board, general nursing and miscellaneous hospital service and supplies.<br>(Reserve days not renewable.) | 1st 60 days<br>61st–90th day<br>91st–150th day<br>Beyond 150 days | All but $676<br>All but $169 per day<br>All but $338 per day<br>No benefits | $676<br>$169 per day<br>$338 per day<br>Entire cost |
| SKILLED NURSING FACILITY CARE<br>You must have been in a hospital for at least 3 days and enter a Medicare-approved facility, generally within 30 days of discharge | 1st 20 days<br>Next 80 days<br>Beyond 100 days | 100 % of approved amount<br>All but $84.50 a day<br>No benefit | $0<br>$84.50 a day<br>Entire cost |
| HOME HEALTH CARE<br>Medically necessary skilled care | Part time care for as long as you meet Medicare conditions | 100% of approved amount; 80% of approved amount for durable medical equipment | Nothing for services; 20% for cost of durable medical equipment |
| HOSPICE CARE<br>Pain relief, symptom management and support services for the terminally ill | If you elect the hospice option and for as long as you meet Medicare inpatient respite care | All but small costs for outpatient drugs and inpatient respite care | Small cost sharing for outpatient drugs and inpatient respite care |
| BLOOD | Unlimited if medically necessary | All but the first 3 pints per calendar year | For first 3 pints unless blood deductible has been met under Part B |

# APPENDIX 2 – SUMMARY OF MEDICARE PART B BENEFITS, 1993

(Source: *The 1993 Guide to Health Insurance for People With Medicare*)

| Services | Benefit | Medicare Pays | You Pay |
|---|---|---|---|
| MEDICAL EXPENSES<br>Doctors' services, inpatient and surgical services and supplies, physical and speech therapy, ambulance, diagnostic tests and more | Medicare pays for medical services in or out of the hospital | 80% of approved amount, after $100 deductible | $100 deductible plus 20% of approved amount if your doctor does not accept assignment |
| CLINICAL LAB SERVICES<br>Blood tests, biopsies, urinalyses, etc. | Unlimited if medically necessary | 100% of approved amount | Nothing |
| HOME HEALTH CARE<br>Medically necessary skilled care | Part-time or intermittent skilled care for as long as you meet conditions for benefits | 100% of approved amount; 80% of approved amount for durable medical equipment | Nothing for services; 20% of approved amount for durable medical equipment |
| OUTPATIENT HOSPITAL<br>Services for the diagnosis or treatment of illness or injury | Unlimited if medically necessary | 80% of approved amount (after deductible) | 20% of billed charges plus deductible if not paid |
| BLOOD | Unlimited if medically necessary | 80% of approved amount, starting with 4th pint | First 3 pints, plus 20% of additional pints (after deductible) |

# GLOSSARY

The following terms are used in this book. Italicized terms in definitions are themselves defined in other glossary entries.

**ADEA (Age Discrimination in Employment Act)** A federal law that prohibits employment discrimination based on age.

**AMERICANS WITH DISABILITIES ACT** A federal law prohibiting discrimination against people with disabilities and calling for access to public transportation for the disabled.

**ATTORNEY-IN-FACT** The person appointed in a *durable power of attorney* to make health-care decisions on behalf of another.

**BENEFICIARY** Person who is named to receive some benefit or money from a legal document such as a *trust*, life insurance policy or *will*.

**CODICIL** A document that revises the provisions of an existing *will*.

**COPAYMENT** That portion of the cost of health care that *Medicare* recipients must pay.

**CUSTODIAL CARE** Nonmedical personal care assistance given to a person who cannot care for him or herself.

**DEDUCTIBLE** The money an insurance beneficiary or *Medicare* recipient pays before being entitled to benefits.

**DEFINED BENEFIT** A pension system where the amount of pension to be paid an employee upon retirement is defined by the terms of the pension.

**DEFINED CONTRIBUTION** A pension system where the employer's contribution to an employee's pension is defined, but the amount that will be paid upon retirement is not fixed.

**DRG (Diagnosis Related Group)** The method by which *Medicare* determines how to pay hospitals for the care of Medicare recipients.

**DURABLE POWER OF ATTORNEY FOR HEALTH CARE** A legal document whereby one person authorizes another to make medical and financial decisions should illness or incapacitation occur.

**ECOA (Equal Credit Opportunities Act)** A federal law that prevents age discrimination in credit.

**EQUITY** Value of that part of real estate an owner has actually paid for and owns. Often it refers to that part of the total mortgage payments already paid, excluding interest, taxes and other fees, plus the down payment and any appreciated value.

**ERISA (Employee Retirement Income Security Act)** A federal law that governs private pension plans.

**ESTATE** All property that a person owns.

**ESTATE PLANNING** Legal steps taken to transfer property after death and to reduce probate and tax costs.

**EXECUTOR** Person or corporation appointed in a *will* or by a court to settle the *estate* of a deceased person.

**FIDUCIARY** Person in a position of trust and confidence; a person who has the duty to act primarily for the benefit of another.

**GUARDIANSHIP** A court procedure where a relative, friend or other person (called the guardian) is appointed by a court to manage the financial or personal affairs of another, called the *ward*.

**HEALTH CARE PROXY** The person appointed in a *durable power of attorney for health care* to make health-care decisions on behalf of another.

**HMO (Health Maintenance Organization)** A health insurance system that controls costs by restricting heath-care delivery to plan-approved health care providers.

**HOSPICE CARE** The treatment of terminally ill patients that concentrates on providing pain control and comfort rather than on curative measures.

**INFORMED CONSENT** A rule that compels health care providers to disclose all pertinent medical information to patients and to receive their consent before rendering treatment.

**INFORMED REFUSAL** The right to refuse medical care.

**INTESTATE**  Not leaving a valid *will*.

**IRA (Individual Retirement Account)**  An account that can provide tax benefits on retirement savings.

**IRREVOCABLE TRUST**  A trust that cannot be changed or canceled after it has been created.

**LIVING (OR INTER VIVOS) TRUST**  A trust that is set up and put into effect while the person who created it is still living.

**LIVING WILL**  A document in which a person, while competent to do so, expresses a wish that his or her life not be prolonged by artificial life support systems if his or her medical condition becomes hopeless.

**MEDICAID**  A federal and state financed health care program for the poor.

**MEDICARE**  A form of national health insurance that primarily benefits those who are age 65 and over.

**MEDIGAP**  Private health insurance designed to pay for health care costs not covered by Medicare.

**NOTICE OF NONCOVERAGE**  A document informing a hospitalized Medicare recipient that benefits are going to cease.

**PART A**  The hospital insurance portion of Medicare.

**PART B**  The general health insurance portion of Medicare.

**PEER REVIEW ORGANIZATION**  The professional group that handles Medicare appeals under Part A.

**PENSION**  A sum of money paid regularly, or in a lump sum, as a retirement benefit.

**PROBATE**  Legal process of establishing the validity of a deceased person's last *will*; commonly refers to the process and laws for settling an *estate*.

**REVERSE MORTGAGE**  A loan paid in periodic payments secured by *equity* in real estate.

**REVOCABLE TRUST**  A trust that can be changed or canceled.

**SOCIAL SECURITY**  A government income supplement program for the retired, the disabled, survivors and dependents.

**SSI (Supplemental Security Income)** An income supplement program for the poor.

**SSA (Social Security Administration)** The agency charged with administering *Social Security.*

**STATE OMBUDSMAN** A state official whose job it is to settle disputes between nursing home patients and nursing homes.

**TESTAMENTARY TRUST** A trust created in a *will* that does not take effect until after the death of the person who created the will.

**TRUST** A legal entity that holds and manages property for the benefit of people named in the trust document.

**WARD** A person whom the law regards as incapable of managing his or her own affairs, and over whom or over whose property a guardian is appointed.

**WILL** A legal document that declares how a person wishes his or her property to be distributed after death.

# BIBLIOGRAPHY

The following books, some of which were used in researching this book, cover issues of concern to senior citizens and their families. Some books listed may be out of print but should be found in your local library.

*The Age Care Sourcebook*, by Jean Crichton. Simon and Schuster, Inc., Simon and Schuster Building, Rockefeller Center, 1230 Avenue of the Americas, New York, NY 10020. 1987. 335 pages. (Out of print.)
Covers a wide variety of topics of interest to seniors and their families, including tips on decision-making and a list of community services.

*Aging and the Law*, by Peter J. Strauss, Robert Wolf and Dana Shilling. Commerce Clearing House, 4025 W. Peterson Ave., Chicago, IL 60646. 1990. 882 pages. $100.00.
For the lawyer in you. This book, written for elder-lawyers, summarizes the field of elder law and describes the different laws and court rulings in different states, as well as providing extensive information on federal rules and statutes.

*Elder Care: Choosing & Financing Long-Term Care*, by Joseph Mathews. Nolo Press, 950 Parker St., Berkeley, CA 94710. 1991. 224 pages. $16.95.
Focuses on issues relevant to families facing the prospect of paying for long-term care. Topics covered include: care in the home, nursing homes, retirement communities and paying for it all.

*The Frugal Shopper,* by Ralph Nader and Wesley J. Smith. Center for the Study of Responsive Law, P.O. Box 19367, Washington, D.C. 20036. 1992. 255 pages. $10.00.

Gives consumer advice on matters ranging from hiring a lawyer, to buying insurance, to dealing with doctors.

*Funerals: Consumers' Last Rights,* by the Editors of Consumer Reports. Consumers Union, 101 Truman Ave., Yonkers, NY 10703. 1977. 239 pages. (Out-of–print).

Even though written more than 15 years ago, this book contains all the consumer advice you will ever need about planning a funeral. From the people who bring you *Consumer Reports* magazine.

*Home-Made Money: Consumer's Guide to Home Equity Conversion,* American Association of Retired Persons, 601 E St., N.W., Washington, D.C. 20049. 1991. 47 pages. Free.

This guide includes descriptions of different types of home equity conversions with an emphasis on reverse mortgages designed to help older Americans who are "house-rich" but "cash-poor."

*How to Use Trusts to Avoid Probate and Taxes: A Guide to Living, Martial, Support, Charitable and Insurance Trusts,* by Theresa Meehan Rudy, Kay Ostberg and Jean Dimeo in association with HALT. Random House, 201 E. 50th St., New York, NY 10022. 1992. 231 pages. $10.00.

As the title suggests, this book provides a complete overview of trusts. Information on "living" and "testamentary" trusts, the pros and cons of each and how to get a trust drafted. State-by-state appendices, tax charts and glossary included.

*Planning for Incapacity,* Legal Counsel for the Elderly, P.O. Box 96474, Washington, D.C. 20090-6474. $5.00.

Contains in-depth information concerning durable power of attorneys and living wills. Updated as needed and comes with "do-it-yourself" forms for the specific state requested.

*The Power of Attorney Book,* by Denis Clifford. Nolo Press, 950 Parker St., Berkeley, CA 94710. 1991. 320 pages. $19.95.

Describes, in a highly readable fashion, the law controlling powers of attorney and provides power of attorney forms that are legal in different jurisdictions.

*Probate: Settling an Estate: A Step-by-Step Guide,* by Kay Ostberg in association with HALT. Random House, 201 E. 50th St., New York, NY 10022. 1990. 162 pages. $8.95.

A "how-to" book for handling probate from start to finish. Includes a list of probate rules and death tax rates for each state and a check list of the tasks that need to be done.

*Retirement Guide: An Overall Plan for a Comfortable Future,* by Henry Hunnisett and Denise Lamaute. Self-Counsel Press, 1704 N. State St., Bellingham, WA 98225. 1990. 272 pages. $9.95.

Covers everything from seniors' activities to the psychology of retirement, family relationships and finances.

*The Rights of Older Persons,* by Robert N. Brown. Southern Illinois University Press, P.O. Box 3697, Carbondale, IL 62902-3697. 1988. 410 pages. $7.95.

Covers social security, supplemental security income, Medicaid, Medicare, pensions and many other issues. Also includes several appendices.

*The Senior Citizens Handbook: A Nuts And Bolts Guide to More Comfortable Living,* by Wesley J. Smith. Price Stern Sloan Publishers, 11150 Olympic Blvd., Ste. 650, Los Angeles, CA 90064. 1989. 213 pages. (Out-of-print.)

This large-print book covers topics such as retirement living, avoiding scams, earning income, widowhood and health care. Introduction by Ralph Nader.

*Social Security, Medicare and Pensions: A Sourcebook for Older Americans,* by Joseph L. Matthews. Nolo Press, 950 Parker St., Berkeley, CA 94710. 1992. 228 pages. $15.95.

Provides an abundance of detail about the subjects listed in its title, presented in an easy-to-read manner.

*The Spices of Life: The Well-Being Handbook for Older Adults,* by Ruth Fort. Center for the Study of Responsive Law, P.O. Box 19367, Washington, D.C. 20036. 1990. 147 pages. $8.00.

Published by Ralph Nader's organization, this book focuses on issues such as "Learning for Living," "Looking for Energy Lifelines" and "Healthy Body; Healthy Minds."

*Successful Aging: A Sourcebook For Older People and Their Families,* by Anne C. Avery. Ballantine Books, 400 Hahn Rd., Westminister, MD 21157. 1987. 526 pages. (Out-of-print.)

Covers issues such as Alzheimer's disease, planning for retirement, preparing for widowhood or divorce, keeping active and independent living.

*Where to Look for Help With a Pension Problem,* Pension Rights Center, 918 16th St., N.W., Ste. 704, Washington, D.C. 20006. 1993. 43 pages. $8.75.

Lists government agencies and private organizations that answer pension questions, as well as legal programs that provide referrals and assist in pension cases.

*Wills: A Do-It-Yourself Guide,* by Theresa Meehan Rudy and Jean Dimeo. HALT – An Organization of Americans for Legal Reform, 1319 F St., N.W., Ste. 300, Washington, D.C. 20004. 1992. 254 pages. $8.95.

Gives advice about what you can give away in a will and how to prepare a will. Sample will clauses and a listing of state laws governing wills also included.

# MEDICARE PEER REVIEW ORGANIZATIONS

Peer Review Organizations (PROs) can answer questions about hospital stays and other Part A insurance services. PROs are who you go to if you wish to appeal a Notice of Noncoverage.

**ALABAMA**
Alabama Quality Assurance
   Foundation, Inc.
600 Beacon Pkwy., W.
   Ste. 600
Birmingham, AL   35209-3154
(800) 288-4992

**ALASKA**
PRO of Washington (PRO for
   Alaska)
10700 Meridian Ave., N.
Ste. #100
Seattle, WA   98133-9008
(800) 445-6941
Anchorage (907) 562-2252

**ARIZONA**
Health Services Advisory
   Group, Inc.
301 E. Bethany Home Rd.
Ste. B-157
Phoenix, AZ   85011
(800) 359-9909

**ARKANSAS**
Arkansas Foundation for
   Medical Care, Inc.
809 Garrison Ave.
P.O. Box 2424
Ft. Smith, AR   72902
(800) 272-5528

**CALIFORNIA**
California Medical Review,
   Inc.
60 Spear St., Ste. 500
San Francisco, CA   94105
(800) 841-1602

**COLORADO**
Colorado Foundation for
   Medical Care
1260 S. Parker Rd.
P.O. Box 17300
Denver, CO   80217-0300
(303) 695-3300

**CONNECTICUT**
Connecticut Peer Review
   Organization, Inc.
100 Roscommon Dr., Ste. 200
Middletown, CT   06457
(203) 632-2008

**DELAWARE**
West Virginia Medical
    Institute, Inc. (PRO for DE)
3001 Chesterfield Pl.
Charleston, WV 25304
(800) 642-8686, Ext. 266

**DISTRICT OF COLUMBIA**
Delmarva Foundation for
    Medical Care, Inc.
9240 Centreville Rd.
Easton, MD 21601
(800) 645-0011

**FLORIDA**
Blue Cross and Blue Shield of
    Florida, Inc.
P.O. Box 2711
Jacksonville, FL 32231
(904) 791-6111

**GEORGIA**
Georgia Medical Care
    Foundation
57 Executive Park South, N.E.
Ste. #200
Atlanta, GA 30329
(404) 982-0411

**HAWAII**
Hawaii Medical Service Assoc.
818 Keeaumoku St.
P.O. Box 860
Honolulu, HI 96808
(808) 944-35861

**IDAHO**
Professional Review Org.
(PRO for Idaho)
10700 Meridian Ave., N.
    Ste. 100
Seattle, WA 98122-9008
(800) 445-6941

**ILLINOIS**
Crescent Counties Foundation
    for Medical Care
280 Shuman Blvd., Ste. 240
Naperville, IL 60563
(800) 647-8089

**INDIANA**
Sentinel Medical Review Org.
2901 Ohio Blvd.
P.O. Box 3713
Terre Haute, IN 47803
(800) 288-1499

**IOWA**
Iowa Foundation for
    Medical Care
6000 Westown Pkwy., Ste. 350-E
W. Des Moines, IA 50266-
    7771
(800) 752-7014

**KANSAS**
The Kansas Foundation for
    Medical Care, Inc.
2947 S.W. Wanamaker Dr.
Topeka, KS 66614
(800) 432-0407

**KENTUCKY**
Sentinel Medical Review Org.
10503 Timberwood Cir., Ste.
    200
P.O. Box 23540
Louisville, KY 40223
(800) 288-1499

**LOUISIANA**
Louisiana Health Care Review
8591 United Plaza Blvd.,
    Ste. 270
Baton Rouge, LA 70809
(504) 926-6353

**MAINE**
Health Care Review, Inc.
(PRO for Maine)
Henry C. Hall Bldg.
345 Blackstone Blvd.
Providence, RI 02906
(401) 331-6661
(800) 541-9888 (RI Only)

**MARYLAND**
Delmarva Foundation for
Medical Care, Inc.
(PRO for Maryland)
9240 Centerville Rd.
Easton, MD 21601
(800) 492-5811

**MASSACHUSETTS**
Massachusetts Peer Review
Organization, Inc.
300 Pearville Rd.
Waltham, MA 02154
(800) 252-5533

**MICHIGAN**
Michigan Peer Review
Organization
40600 Ann Arbor Rd., Ste. 200
Plymouth, MI 48710
(800) 365-5899

**MINNESOTA**
Foundation for Health Care
Evaluation
2901 Metro Dr., Ste. 400
Bloomington, MN 55425
(800) 444-3423

**MISSISSIPPI**
Mississippi Foundation for
Medical Care, Inc.
735 Riverside Dr.
P.O. Box 4665
Jackson, MS 39296-4665
(800) 844-0600

**MISSOURI**
Missouri Patient Care Review
Foundation
505 Hobbs Rd., Ste. 100
Jefferson City, MO 65109
(800) 347-1016

**MONTANA**
Montana-Wyoming
Foundation for Medical
Care
400 North Park, 2nd Fl.
Helena, MT 59601
(406) 443-4020
(800) 497-8232 (MT Only)

**NEBRASKA**
Iowa Foundation for Care
(PRO for Nebraska)
6000 Westown Pkwy., Ste. 350-E
W. Des Moines, IA 50266-
7771
(800) 247-3004

**NEVADA**
Nevada Peer Review
675 E. 2100 South, Suite 270
Salt Lake City, UT 84106
(800) 558-0829

**NEW HAMPSHIRE**
New Hampshire Foundation
for Medical Care
15 Old Rollinsford Rd.
Dover, NH 03820
(800) 582-7174 (NH only)

**NEW JERSEY**
The Peer Review Organization
of New Jersey, Inc.
Brier Hill Ct., Bldg. J
East Brunswick, NJ 08816
(908) 238-5570
(800) 624-4557 (NJ Only)

**NEW MEXICO**
New Mexico Medical Review
 Association
707 Broadway, N.E., Ste. 200
P.O. Box 27449
Albuquerque, NM 87125-7449
(505) 842-6236
800) 432-6824 (NM Only)

**NEW YORK**
Island Peer Review
 Organization, Inc.
1979 Marcus Ave., 1st Fl.
Lake Success, NY 11042
(800) 331-7767

**NORTH CAROLINA**
Medical Medical Review of
 North Carolina
1011 Schaub Dr., Ste. 200
P.O. Box 37309
Raleigh, NC 27627
(919) 851-2955
(800) 682-2650 (NC Only)

**NORTH DAKOTA**
North Dakota Health Care
 Review, Inc.
900 N. Broadway, Ste. 301
Minot, ND 58701
(701) 852-4231
(800) 472-2902 (ND Only)

**OHIO**
Peer Review Systems, Inc.
757 Brooksedge Plaze Dr.
P.O. Box 6174
Westerville, OH 43081-6174
(800) 233-7337

**OKLAHOMA**
Oklahoma Foundation for
 Peer Review, Inc.
The Paragon Bldg.
5801 Broadway Extension
 Ste. #400
Oklahoma City, OK 73118-
 7489
(405) 840-2891
(800) 522-3414 (OK Only)

**OREGON**
Oregon Medical Professional
 Review Organization
1220 S.W. Morrison, #200
Portland, OR 97205
(800) 344-4354 (OR only)

**PENNSYLVANIA**
Keystone Peer Review
 Organization, Inc.
P.O. Box 8310
Harrisburg, PA 17105-8310
(717) 564-8288
(800) 322-1914 (PA Only)

**PUERTO RICO**
Puerto Rico Foundation for
 Medical Care
Mercantile Plaza, Ste. 605
Hato Rei, PR 00918
(809) 753-6705

**RHODE ISLAND**
Health Care Review Inc.
Henry C. Hall Bldg.
345 Blackstone Blvd.
Providence, RI 02906
(401) 331-6661
(800) 662-5028 (RI Only)

**SOUTH CAROLINA**
Carolina Medical Review
101 Executive Center Dr.,
 Ste. 123
Columbia, SC 29210
(803) 731-8225
(800) 922-3089 (SC Only)

**SOUTH DAKOTA**
South Dakota Foundation for
Medical Care
1323 South Minnesota Ave.
Sioux Falls, SD 57105
(605) 336-3505
(800) 658-2285 (SD Only)

**TENNESSEE**
Mid-South Foundation for
Medical Care
6401 Poplar Ave., Ste. 400
Memphis, TN 38119
(901) 682-0381
(800) 873-2273 (TN Only)

**TEXAS**
Texas Medical Foundation
Barton Oaks Plaza Two
901 Mopac Expressway, S.,
Ste. 200
Austin, TX 78746
(512) 329-6610

**UTAH**
Utah Peer Review
Organization
675 East 2100 South, Ste. 270
Salt Lake City, UT 84106
(800) 274-2290

**VERMONT**
Peer Review Organization for
Vermont
31 Hercules Dr.
Gilchester, VT 05446
(802) 655-6302
(800) 639-8427

**VIRGINIA**
Medical Society of Virginia
Review Organization
1604 Santa Rosa Rd., Ste. 200
P.O. Box K-70
Richmond, VA 23288
(800) 545- 3814 (DC, MD &
VA)

**WASHINGTON**
Professional Review
Organization for
Washington
10700 Meridian Ave., N.,
Ste. 100
Seattle, WA 98133-9008
(800) 445-6941

**WEST VIRGINIA**
West Virginia Medical
Institute
3001 Chesterfield Pl.
Charleston, WV 25304
(800) 642-8686, Ext. 266

**WISCONSIN**
Wisconsin Peer Review
Organization
2909 Landmark Pl.
Madison, WI 53713
(800) 362-2320

**WYOMING**
Montana-Wyoming
Foundation for Medical
Care
400 North Park, 2nd Fl.
Helena, MT 59601
(406) 443-4020
(800) 497-8232

# MEDICARE CARRIERS

Carriers can answer questions about Medicare Part B.

**ALABAMA**
Medicare/Blue Cross & Blue
  Shield of Alabama
P.O. Box 830-140
Birmingham, AL    35283-0140
(800) 292-8855

**ALASKA**
Medicare/Aetna Life &
  Casualty
200 S.W. Market St.
P.O. Box 1997
Portland, OR  97207-1997
(503) 222- 6831

**ARIZONA**
Medicare/Aetna Life &
  Casualty
P.O. Box 37200
Phoenix, AZ  85069
(602) 861-1968
(800) 352-0411 (AZ Only)

**ARKANSAS**
Medicare/Arkansas Blue
  Cross & Blue Shield
P.O. Box 1418
Little Rock, AR  72203-1418
(501) 378-2173 (Hospital)
(501) 378-2320 (Physician)
(800) 482- 5525 (AR Only)

**CALIFORNIA**
Counties of L.A., Orange, San
  Diego,Ventura,  Imperial,
  San Luis Obispo, Santa
  Barbara
Medicare/Transamerica
  Occidental Life Insurance
  Co.
Box 50061
Upland, CA  91785-5061
(714) 985-9801
Rest of CA: Medicare Claims
  Dept.,
Blue Shield of California
Chico, CA  95976
(916) 891-1006
(800) 952-8627 or (800) 848-7713
  (CA Only)

**COLORADO**
Medicare/Blue Cross & Blue
  Shield of Colorado
Coordination of Benefits:
P.O. Box 173550
Correspondence Appeals:
P.O. Box 173500
Denver, CO  80217
(800) 331-6175

**CONNECTICUT**
Medicare/The Travelers Co.
538 Preston Ave.
P.O. Box 9000
Meriden, CT  06454-9000
(203) 639-3000
(800) 982-6819 (CT Only)

**DELAWARE**
Medicare/Pennsylvania Blue
  Shield
P.O. Box 890200
Camp Hill, PA  17089-0200
(800) 233-1124

**DISTRICT OF COLUMBIA**
Medicare/Pennsylvania Blue
  Shield
P.O. Box 890100
Camp Hill, PA  17089-0100
(800) 233-1124

**FLORIDA**
Medicare/Blue Shield of
  Florida, Inc.
P.O. Box 2525
Jacksonville, FL  32231
(800) 666-7586

**GEORGIA**
Medicare/Aetna Life and
  Casualty
P.O. Box 3018
Savannah, GA  31402-3018
(800) 727-0827

**HAWAII**
Medicare/Aetna Life &
  Casualty
P.O. Box 3947
Honolulu, HI  96812
(808) 524-1240
(800) 272-5242 (HI Only)

**IDAHO**
EQUICOR/CIGNA
3150 N. Lakeharbor Ln., Ste.
  254
Boise, ID  83707-6219
(800) 627-2782 (ID Only)

**ILLINOIS**
Medicare Claims/Blue Cross
  & Blue Shield of Illinois
P.O. Box 4422
Marion, IL  62959
(800) 642-6930 (IL Only)

**INDIANA**
Medicare Part B/AdminaStar
  Federal
P.O. Box 7073
Indianapolis, IN  46207
(800) 622-4792

**IOWA**
Medicare/IASD Health
  Services, Inc.
636 Grand Ave.
Des Moines, IA  50309
(800) 532-1285

**KANSAS**
Counties of Johnson,
  Wyandotte
Medicare/Blue Cross & Blue
  Shield of Kansas City
P.O. Box 419840
Kansas City, MO  64141-6840
(816) 561-0900
Rest of State: Medicare/Blue
Cross & Blue Shield of Kansas
P.O. Box 239
Topeka, KS  66601
(913) 232-3773
(800) 432-3531 (KS Only)

**KENTUCKY**
Medicare Part B/ Blue Shield
  of Kentucky
100 East Vine St.
Lexington, KY 40507
(800) 999-7608

**LOUISIANA**
Arkansas Blue Cross and Blue
  Shield Medicare Adm.
P.O. Box 83830
Baton Rouge, LA 70884-3830
(800) 462-9666 (LA Only)

**MAINE**
Medicare B/C and S
  Administrative Services
P.O. Box 9790
Portland, MN 04104-5090
(800) 462-9666 (MN Only)

**MARYLAND**
Counties of Montgomery &
  Prince Georges
Medicare/Pennsylvania Blue
  Shield
P.O. Box 890100
Camp Hill, PA 17089-0100
(800) 233-1124
Rest of State:
Maryland Blue Cross & Blue
  Shield, Inc.
1946 Greenspring Dr.
Timonium, MD 21093
(410) 561-4160
(800) 492-4795 (MD Only)

**MASSACHUSETTS**
Medicare B/C and S
  Administration Services
1022 Hingham St.
Rockland, MA 02371
(800) 882-1228 (MA Only)

**MICHIGAN**
Medicare Part B
Michigan Blue Cross & Blue
  Shield
P.O. Box 2201
Detroit, MI 48231
(313) 225-8200
(800) 482-4045
(800) 322-0607 (In Area Code
  517 only)
(800) 442-8020 (In Area Code
  616 only)
(800) 562-7802 (In Area Code
  906 only)

**MINNESOTA**
Counties of: Anoka, Dakota,
  Filmore, Goodhue,
  Hennepin, Houston,
  Olmstead, Ramsey,
  Wabasha, Washington,
  Winona
Medicare/The Travelers Ins.
  Co.
8120 Penn Ave., South
Bloomington, MN 55431
(800) 352-2762 (MN Only)
Rest of State: Medicare/Blue
  Shield of Minnesota
P.O. Box 64357
St. Paul, MN 55164
(612) 456-8000

**MISSISSIPPI**
Medicare/The Travelers Ins.
  Co.
P.O. Box 22545
Jackson, MS 39225-2545
(601) 977-5855
(800 227-2349

## MISSOURI
Counties of Andrew, Atchison,
Bates, Benton, Buchanan,
Caldwell, Carroll, Cass,
Clay, Clinton, Daviess,
DeKalb, Gentry, Grundy,
Harrison, Henry, Holt,
Jackson, Johnson,
Lafayette, Livingston,
Mercer, Nodaway, Pettis,
Platte, Ray, St. Clair,
Saline,Vernon, Worth
Medicare/Blue Shield of
Kansas City
P.O. Box 419840
Kansas City, MO 64141-6840
(816) 561-0900
(800) 892-5900 (MO Only)
Rest of State:
Medicare/General Amercan
Life Ins. Co.
P.O. Box 505
St. Louis, MO 63166
(314) 843-8880
(800) 392-3070 (MO Only)

## MONTANA
Medicare/Blue Cross and Blue
Shield of Montana
P.O. Box 4310
Helena, MT 59604
(406) 444-8350
(800) 332-6146 (MT Only)

## NEBRASKA
Blue Shield of Kansas
Medicare Part B
Blue Cross/Blue Shield of
Kansas
P.O. Box 3106
Omaha, NE 68103-0106
(913) 232-3773
(800) 633-1113 (NE Only)

## NEVADA
Medicare/Aetna Life &
Casualty
P.O. Box 37230
Phoenix, AZ 85069
(602) 861-1968
(800) 528-0311 (AZ Only)

## NEW HAMPSHIRE
Medicare B/C and S
Administrative Services
P.O. Box 9790
Portland, MN 04104-5090
(800) 447-1142 (NH Only)

## NEW JERSEY
Medicare/Pennsylvania Blue
Shield
P.O. Box 400010
Harrisburg, PA 17140-0010
(717) 763-3601
(800) 462-9306 (PA Only)

## NEW MEXICO
Medicare/Aetna Life and
Casualty
P.O. Box 25500
Oklahoma City, OK 73125-
0500
(800) 423-2925

## NEW YORK
Counties of: Bronx, Kings,
New York, Richmond,
Columbia, Delaware,
Dutchess, Greene, Nassau,
Orange, Putnam,
Rockland, Suffolk, Sullivan,
Ulster, Westchester:
Medicare B/Blue Cross & Blue
Shield
P.O. Box 2280
Peekskill, NY 10566
(516) 244-5100 or (800) 442-8430

County of Queens:
  Medicare/Group Health,
  Inc.
Ansonia Station
P.O. Box 1608
New York, NY 10023
(212) 721-1770
Rest of state:
Medicare Blue Shield of
  Western New York
7-9 Court St.
Binghamton, NY 13901-3197
(607) 772-9264
(800) 252-6550 (NY Only)

**NORTH CAROLINA**
Connecticut General Life
  Insurance Company
P.O. Box 671
Nashville, TN 37202
(800) 672-3071

**NORTH DAKOTA**
Medicare/Blue Shield of
  North Dakota
4510 13th Ave., S.W.
Fargo, ND 58121-0001
(800) 247-2267

**OHIO**
Medicare/Nationwide Mutual
  Insurance Co.
Columbus, OH 43216
(614) 249-7157
(800) 282-0530 (OH Only)

**OKLAHOMA**
Medicare/Aetna Life and
  Casualty
701 N.W. 63rd St.
Oklahoma City, OK 73116
(800) 522-9079

**OREGON**
Medicare/Aetna Life &
  Casualty
200 S.W. Market St.
P.O. Box 1997
Portland, OR 97207-1997
(503) 221-5535

**PENNSYLVANIA**
Medicare/Pennsylvania Blue
  Shield
P.O. Box 890065
Camp Hill, PA 17089-0065
(800) 233-1124

**RHODE ISLAND**
Medicare/Blue Cross & Blue
  Shield of Rhode Island
444 Westminster St.
Providence, RI 02903-3279
(800) 662-5170

**SOUTH CAROLINA**
Medicare Part B
Blue Cross & Blue Shield of
  South Carolina
Fontaine Road Business Ctr.
300 Arbor Lake Dr., Ste. 1300
Columbia, SC 29223
(800) 868-2522

**SOUTH DAKOTA**
Medicare Part B/Blue Shield
  of North Dakota
4510 13th Ave., S.W.
Fargo, ND 58121-0001
(800) 247-2267

**TENNESSEE**
Connecticut Mutual
P.O. Box 1465
Nashville, TN 37202
(615) 665-1030
(800) 342-8900 (TN Only)

**TEXAS**
Medicare/Blue Cross & Blue
   Shield of Texas, Inc.
P.O. Box 660031
Dallas, TX  75266-0031
(214) 470-0222
(800) 442-2620 (TX Only)

**UTAH**
Medicare/Blue Cross & Blue
   Shield of Utah
P.O. Box 30269
Salt Lake City, UT  84130-0269
(801) 487-6441
(800) 426-3477 (UT Only)

**VERMONT**
Medicare B/C and S
   Administrative Services
P.O. Box 9790
Portland, ME  04104-5090
(800) 447-1142 (VT Only)

**VIRGINIA**
Counties of: Arlington,
   Fairfax
Medicare/Pennsylvania Blue
   Shield
P.O. Box 890100
Camp Hill, PA  17089-0100
(717) 763-3601
Rest of state:
Medicare/The Travelers Ins.
   Co.
P.O. Box 26463

Richmond, VA  23261
(804) 330-4786
(800) 552-3423 (VA Only)

**WASHINGTON**
Washington State Medicare B
P.O. Box 91070
Seattle, WA  98111-9170
In Seattle (800) 422-4087
In Spokane (800) 572-5256
In Tacoma (206) 597-6530

**WEST VIRGINIA**
Medicare/Nationwide Mutual
   Insurance Co.
P.O. Box 57
Columbus, OH  43216
(614) 249-7157
(800) 848-0106 (WV Only)

**WISCONSIN**
Medicare/Wisconsin
   Physician Service (WPS)
P.O. Box 1787
Madison, WI  53701
(608) 221-3330
(800) 362-7221 (WI Only)

**WYOMING**
Blue Cross & Blue Shield
   of Wyoming
P.O. Box 628
Cheyenne, WY  82003
(307) 634-1393
(800) 442-2371 (WY Only)

# STATE AGENCIES ON AGING

The offices listed in this section are responsible for coordinating services for older Americans:

**ALABAMA**
Commission on Aging
RSA Plaza
770 Washington Ave., Ste. 470
Montomery, AL 36130
(205) 242-5743
(800) 243-5463 (AL Only)

**ALASKA**
Older Alaskans Commission
P.O. Box 110209
Juneau, AK 99811-0209
(907) 465-3250

**ARIZONA**
Department of Economic
  Security
Aging and Adult Admin.
1789 West Jefferson, Cycle
  950A
Phoenix, AZ 85007
(602) 542-4446

**ARKANSAS**
Division of Aging and Adult
  Services
Donaghey Plaza South
7th & Main St., Ste. 1417
Little Rock, AR 72203-1437
(501) 682-2441

**CALIFORNIA**
Department of Aging
1600 K St.
Sacramento, CA 95814
(916) 322-3887

**COLORADO**
Aging and Adult Services
Department of Social Services
1575 Sherman St., 4th Fl.
Denver, CO 80203-1714
(303) 866-3851

**CONNECTICUT**
Department of Aging
175 Main St.
Hartford, CT 06106
(203) 566-3238
(800) 443-9946 (CT Only)

**DELAWARE**
Division of Aging,
  Department of Health and
  Social Services
Main Bldg., Annex, 2nd Fl.
1901 N. DuPont Hwy.
New Castle, DE 19720
(302) 577-4660
(800) 223-9074 (New Castle)
(800) 292-1515 (Melford)

**DISTRICT OF COLUMBIA**
Office of Aging
1424 K Street, N.W., 2nd Fl.
Washington, DC  20005
(202) 724-5626

**FLORIDA**
Office of Aging and Adult
    Services
1317 Winewood Blvd.
Tallahassee, FL  32311
(904) 488-8922

**GEORGIA**
Office of Aging
Department of Human
    Resources
878 Peachtree St., N.E., Rm.
    632
Atlanta, GA  30309
(404) 894-5333

**HAWAII**
Executive Office on Aging
335 Merchant St., Ste. 241
Honolulu, HI  96813
(808) 586-0100

**IDAHO**
Office on Aging
Statehouse, Rm. 108
Boise, ID  83720
(208) 334-3833

**ILLINOIS**
Department on Aging
421 E. Capitol Ave.
Springfield, IL  62701
(217) 785-2870

**INDIANA**
Department of Human Services
Office of Aging
402 W. Washington
P.O. Box 7083
Indianapolis, IN  46207-7083
(317) 232-7020

**IOWA**
Department of Elder Affairs
Jewett Building
914 Grand Ave., Ste. 236
Des Moines, IA  50319
(515) 281-5187
(800)-532-3213 (Nursing Home
    Complaints)

**KANSAS**
Department on Aging
122 S. Docking State Office
    Bldg.
915 S.W. Harrison
Topeka, KS  66612-1500
(913) 296-4986
(800)-432-3535

**KENTUCKY**
Division for Aging Services
Department of Social Services
275 E. Main St.
Frankfort, KY  40621
(502) 564-6930

**LOUISIANA**
Governor's Office of Elderly
    Affairs
P.O. Box 80374
Baton Rouge, LA  70898-0374
(504) 925-1700

**MAINE**
Bureau of Elder & Adult
    Services
35 Anthony Ave., Ste. 11
Augusta, ME  04333
(207) 624-5335

**MARYLAND**
State Agency on Aging
301 W. Preston St., Rm. 1004
Baltimore, MD  21201
(410) 225-1102
(800)-243-3425 (MD Only)

**MASSACHUSETTS**
Executive Office of Elder
  Affairs
One Ashburton Pl.
Boston, MA 02118
(617) 727-7750

**MICHIGAN**
Office of Services to the Aging
P.O. Box 30026
Lansing, MI 48909
(517) 373-8230

**MINNESOTA**
Minnesota Board on Aging
Human Services Bldg.
444 Lafayette Rd.
St. Paul, MN 55155-3843
(612) 296-2544
(800) 657-3591 (MN Only)

**MISSISSIPPI**
Council on Aging
455 N. Lamont St.
Jackson, MS 39202
(601) 359-6770

**MISSOURI**
Division of Aging
Department of Social Services
P.O. Box 1337
615 Howerton Ct.
Jefferson, MO 65102-1337
(314) 751-3082
(800) 392-3082 (Elder Abuse
  Hotline)
(800) 235-5503 (Referral
  Hotline)

**MONTANA**
The Governor's Office on
  Aging
State Capital Building
Helena, MT 59620-0801
(406) 444-3111
(800) 332-2272 (Citizen's
  Advocate Office, MT Only)

**NEBRASKA**
Department of Aging
State Office Bldg.
301 Centennial Mall S.
Lincoln, NE 68509
(402) 471-2306
(800)-942-7830 (NE Only)

**NEVADA**
Department of Human
  Resources
Division for Aging Services
1665 Hot Springs Rd., Ste. 158
Carson City, NV 89706
(702) 687-4210

**NEW HAMPSHIRE**
Department of Health and
  Human Services
Division of Elderly Services
State Office Park S., Bldg. #1
115 Pleasant St.
Concord, NH 03301
(603) 271-4680
(800) 852-3345
(800) 442-5640
(800) 351-1888, Ext.4687
(Alzheimer's Hotline)

**NEW JERSEY**
Dept. of Community Affairs
Division on Aging
101 S. Broad & Front St., CN
  807
Trenton, NJ 08625-0807
(609) 292-4833
(800) 792-8820 (NJ Only)

**NEW MEXICO**
Agency on Aging
La Villa Rivera Bldg.
  Ground Fl.
224 E. Palace Ave.
Santa Fe, NM 87501
(505) 827-7640
(800) 432-2080 (NM Only)

**NEW YORK**
State Office for the Aging
2 Empire State Plaza
Albany, NY 12223-0001
(518) 474-5731
(800) 342-9871 (NY Only)

**NORTH CAROLINA**
Department of Human
    Resources
Division of Aging
693 Palmer Dr.
Caller Box 29531
Raleigh, NC 27626-0531
(919) 733-3983
(800) 662-7030 (Care Line)

**NORTH DAKOTA**
Department of Human Services
Aging Services Division
State Capitol Bldg.
P.O. Box 7070
Bismarck, ND 58507
(701) 224-2577

**OHIO**
Department of Aging
50 W. Broad St., 8th Fl.
Columbus, OH 43266-0501
(614) 466-1221

**OKLAHOMA**
Department of Human Services
Aging Services Division
P.O. Box 25352
Oklahoma, City, OK 73125
(405) 521-2327

**OREGON**
Department of Human
    Resources
Senior Services Division
500 Summers St., N.E., 2nd Fl.
Salem, OR 97310-1015
(800) 232-3020 (Program Help)
(800) 282-8096
    (Administration)

**PENNSYLVANIA**
Department of Aging
Barto Bldg.
231 State St.
Harrisburg, PA 17101
(717) 783-1550

**RHODE ISLAND**
Department of Elderly Affairs
160 Pine St.
Providence, RI 02903
(401) 277-2858

**SOUTH CAROLINA**
Commission on Aging
400 Arbor Lake Dr., Ste. B-500
Columbia, SC 29223
(803) 735-0210

**SOUTH DAKOTA**
Agency on Aging
Adult Services and Aging
Richard F. Kneip Bldg.
700 Governors Dr.
Pierre, SD 57501-2291
(605) 773-3656

**TENNESSEE**
Commission on Aging
706 Church St., Ste. 201
Nashville, TN 37243-0860
(615) 741-2056

**TEXAS**
Department on Aging
Capitol Station
P.O. Box 12786
Austin, TX 78711
(512) 444-2727
(800) 252-9240 (Gen. Info.,
    TX Only)
(800) 252-2412 (Nursing,
    TX Only)

**UTAH**
Division of Aging and Adult
  Services
120 North 200 West, Ste. 401
Salt Lake City, UT 84103
(801) 538-3910

**VERMONT**
Office on Aging
Waterbury Complex
103 S. Main St.
Waterbury, VT 05671-2301
(802) 241-2400

**VIRGINIA**
Department for the Aging
700 E. Franklin St., 10th Fl.
Richmond, VA 23219-2327
(804) 225-2271
(800)552-4464 (Gen. Info., VA
  Only)
(800)552-3402 (Long Term
  Care, VA Only)

**WASHINGTON**
Aging & Adult Services
  Administration
Department of Social and
  Health Services
P.O. Box 45050
Olympia, WA 98504-5050
(206) 586-3768
(800) 422-3563 (Hotline)
(800) 582-6078 (Nursing Home
  Complaints)

**WEST VIRGINIA**
Commission on Aging
State Capitol Complex, Holly
  Grove
1900 Canal Blvd.
Charleston, WV 25305
(304) 558-3317

**WISCONSIN**
Bureau on Aging
Department of Health and
  Human Services
P.O. Box 7851
Madison, WI 53707
(608) 266-2536

**WYOMING**
Commission on Aging
Hathaway Building, 1st Fl.
Cheyenne, WY 82002
(307) 777-7986
(800)442-2766 (WY Only)

# NATIONAL ORGANIZATIONS

The following is a list of national organizations which work on behalf of seniors. Contact the organization if you would like more information on the services they offer.

American Association of
Retired Persons (AARP)
AARP National Headquarters
601 E St., N.W.
Washington, D.C.   20049
(202) 434-2277

The National Council on the
Aging
409 3rd St., S.W., Ste. 200
Washington, D.C.   20024
(202) 479-1200

The National Council of
Senior Citizens
1331 F St., N.W.
Washington, D.C.   20004
(202) 347-8800

The National Institute on
Aging
NIA Information Center
P.O. Box 8057
Gaithersburg, MD   20879-8057
(301) 587-2528

The National Senior Citizens
Law Center
1815 H St., N.W., Ste. 700
Washington, D.C.   20006
(202) 887-5280

The Older Women's League
666 11th St., N.W., Ste. 700
Washington, D.C.   20001
(202) 783-6686

Pension Rights Center
918 16th St., N.W.
Washington, D.C.   20006
(202) 296-3776

# MEDICARE SUPPLEMENT INSURANCE COUNSELING

Some states have counseling services for seniors who are thinking of buying Medigap insurance. Here are the phone numbers of those states that offer the service.

**CALIFORNIA**
(800) 927-4357

**DELAWARE**
(302) 739-4251

**FLORIDA**
(800) 342-2762

**IDAHO**
(208) 334-2250

**ILLINOIS**
(217) 782-0004

**INDIANA**
(800) 622-4461

**IOWA**
(515) 281-5705

**MARYLAND**
(800) 243-3425

**MASSACHU-SETTS**
(617) 727-7750

**MICHIGAN**
(517) 377-1935

**MISSOURI**
(800) 726-7390

**NEW JERSEY**
(800) 792-8820

**NEW MEXICO**
(800) 432-2080

**NEW YORK**
(800) 342-9871

**NORTH CAROLINA**
(919) 733-0111

**OHIO**
(800) 686-1526

**OREGON**
(800) 722-4138

**TENNESSEE**
(800) 252-2816

**TEXAS**
(512) 463-6515

**VERMONT**
(802) 828-3301

**WASHINGTON**
(206) 586-7441

**WISCONSIN**
(800) 242-1060

## About the Author

Wesley J. Smith is an author, a consumer advocate and an attorney. He is the author of *The Lawyer Book, The Doctor Book,* and *The Senior Citizens' Handbook.* He has coauthored two books with Ralph Nader, *Winning the Insurance Game* and *The Frugal Shopper.* Smith and Nader's next collaboration is *Collision Course: The Truth About Airline Safety,* to be published in fall 1993. Smith is also a lecturer and media commentator, having appeared before community groups, professional associations and educational gatherings across the nation.

## About HALT

HALT — An Organization of Americans for Legal Reform is a national, non-profit, non-partisan public-interest group of more than 100,000 members. It is dedicated to enabling all people to dispose of their legal affairs simply, affordably and equitably. HALT pursues an ambitious program to improve the quality, reduce the cost and increase the accessibility of the civil legal system.

HALT pursues advocacy at the state and federal levels. In particular, HALT supports:

- Reforming "unauthorized practice of law" (UPL) rules that forbid nonlawyers from handling even routine uncontested matters, limit consumers' options and make legal services unaffordable to many.

- Assuring consumer protection against incompetence and fraud by replacing lawyer self-regulation with public control and accountability in systems for disciplining lawyers and judges.

- Developing standardized do-it-yourself forms and simplified procedures for routine legal matters such as wills, uncontested divorces, trusts and simple bankruptcies.

- Creating pro-consumer alternatives to the tort system, such as alternative-compensation systems that guarantee swift and fair compensation for those injured.

To achieve its educational goals, HALT publishes Citizens Legal Manuals like this one and an "Everyday Law Series" of brief legal guides to increase consumers' ability to handle their own legal affairs and help them become better-informed users of legal services. Written in easy-to-understand language, these materials explain basic legal principles and procedures, including step-by-step "how-to" instructions.

HALT's quarterly publication, *The Legal Reformer,* is the only national periodical of legal reform news and analysis. It informs readers about major legal reform developments and what they can do to help.

HALT's activities are funded primarily through member contributions.